Pure Genius

Simple Solutions That Work To Light Up Your World

Introduction by

Eiji Morishita

www.geniussquared.com

Copyright Text

Published by Motivational Press, Inc.
2360 Corporate Circle
Suite 400
Henderson, NV 89074
www.MotivationalPress.com

www.geniussquared.com

Manufactured in the United States of America.

ISBN: 978-1-935723-97-4

"Pure Genius, is just that, pure genius, the insights that the experts bring to the table really get you thinking in a different direction. If you are looking to grow your business and have more success in your life these simple solutions will help you do that. I was particularly drawn to the idea of knowing yourself and knowing your innate needs and what is really driving you. The exercises outlined in this chapter allow you to access the power from within and know what you are driven by so that you can reach your needs and start living the life you want to live."

– **Kim Beckers**, Strategic Success Coach & Certified
Online Business Manager, http://www.kimbeckers.com

"Eiji Morishita has pulled together an array of works to remind us all of our own genius and how we can bring it out to share with the world."

– **Robin Colucci**, Author How to Write a Book that Sells:
5 Steps to Become a Credible Expert

"PURE GENIUS is one of those rare finds that not only opens your mind to new ideas, but opens your heart to new ways of feeling. There are pieces of wisdom in each chapter, which keeps me coming back for more!"

– **Lisa Jones**, Author of Art of Living Happy.
http://www.artoflivinghappy.com

"In Eiji Morishita's collaborative work, Pure Genius, excellence and energy jump off every page. And if you're smart, you'll try to absorb every word. Genius is something above and beyond the ordinary. When exceptional people do exceptional work, you want to know about it, learn it, absorb it. When you're around people who embody genius, you are drawn to them; Geniuses are those who stand apart and are powerfully different, and you want them to rub off on you. That is what happens when reading Pure Genius: you're so magnetized by the various authors' brilliance that you don't want to stop reading. You want to rub elbows with them, in the hopes that some of it will rub off. Eiji has brought together some of the finest minds in their fields, people who know how to translate their particular genius in a digestible, understandable way. I suggest you devour it and let it rub off on you, page by quickly-turning-page."

– **Teri Goetz**, CPC, MS, L.Ac., Mentor, Guide and
Soul Purpose Coach for Women, http://www.terigoetz.com

CONTENTS

ACKNOWLEDGEMENTS

Sending out thanks and gratitude to all the geniuses past and present who made this book possible. It was made achievable by being able to stand on the shoulders of the giants who went before us: (Partial list) Albert Einstein, Mahatma Gandhi, Thomas Edison, Nikola Tesla, Benjamin Franklin, Mother Theresa, Dalai Lama, Jesus Christ, Buddha, Walt Disney, Steve Jobs, Andrew Carnegie, Oprah, Leonardo Da Vinci, Michelangelo, Martin Luther King Jr, Julius Caesar, Princess Di, and Nelson Mandela.

DEDICATION

This book is dedicated to the genius within you. Genius is not about IQ but a level of performance beyond mastery. You have genius inside you and a powerful message the world needs to hear. Our intention is to give you permission to shine your light and your wisdom to the world.

FOREWORD

Dig up your GENIUS
by Bernice Coles

I was born in a very small town in West Virginia. To this day that town ONLY has one road. Yep. It has one, very, very long road. When I was small it was a dusty, gravel strewn road, with well worn grooves. I have vivid memories of huge dump trucks rumbling down that road. The trucks would lurch, and lumber along, creaking beneath the weight of their load. The trucks would make several trips out of that holler with the contents piled high. Pitch black, shiny in places and hard to come by. There is a coal mine at the end of that road. Coal is like Genius.

Genius is often hidden, it needs to be mined for, excavated, and often risks have to be taken. There may even be dark times which need to be illuminated by those who can light the way. Coal was in those dump trucks and it's a natural, raw material which has to be dug up, stripped off, processed and *then* utilized. How similar we are with Genius inside? Mining is risky business. At times, mining for Genius may be risky too. Everyone has Genius, but it takes the pros to really unearth the rich deposit that's inside us all. You don't come to the planet empty. You have value. You have worth. You can shine because you have Pure Genius.

Bernice Coles is a speaker, author, and creative thinker. As she moved toward her highest Genius Coles taught elementary school, worked as a senior media relations assistant for the Johns Hopkins School of Medicine Office of Public Affairs, and was a recruiter and program manager for a private college. Her Genius shines best when she is speaking, teaching and depositing the richness of her life, her experience and her passion which is to help others discover and develop their life's purpose. Coles motivates and inspires audiences to use their giftedness doing work they love.

INTRODUCTION

by **Eiji Morishita**

**"The World Is Drowning In Information Yet
Dying of Thirst For Wisdom.
Be the Solution." – Eiji Morishita**

Welcome to PURE GENIUS. First, I want to thank and acknowledge you for taking time out to open the cover. My intention is for you to get the most out of this groundbreaking book which is intended to be fun, simple, empowering, easy to implement and life-changing.

YOUR GENIUS = PASSION + TALENTS + SKILLS + LIFE EXPERIENCES

No one has the same unique combination of your passion, talents, skills, and life experiences. There will be no one like you in the past and no one like you in the future. No two geniuses are alike. You will notice each chapter will have its own unique individual style of each author sharing their genius.

You are unique and have genius inside of you and a powerful message that the world needs to hear. Geniuses play at what others call work. What comes easy for you but hard for others is *your* genius. When you can do it well and make it look easy, you can be handsomely rewarded in the marketplace. The featured authors in this book have been hand selected to showcase their genius and impart their wisdom to you with practical bite sized nuggets of wisdom that you can use to make an impact and light up your world. The world is your playground. Come and play!

First, before we get started, why do you want to read this book? What do you want to get out of it? By knowing your purpose and outcome of why you want to read this, your mind will open up and get clear on what to look for.

Also by knowing your *why*, it'll keep you motivated and inspired to follow through and enjoy the book even more fully.

The fact that you're reading this right now means that you are a genius and you're ready to unlock your genius to tap into the magic of life.

Ground Rules –
When You Know the Rules to the Game, It's Easier to Win

1. Focus on progress not perfection.
Each chapter can stand alone and be read individually. However, to get the most out of the book keep moving through the chapters, it's going to be a fun ride. Enjoy the journey along the way by focusing on progress not perfection, because everything you do is perfect. Billions of things had to happen perfectly for you to be where you are right now.

2. Have fun.
Life is a game and is an enjoyable journey. Movies are better when you suspend disbelief and use your imagination. So sit back, relax, enjoy the ride and suspend disbelief.

3. Suspend judgment.
Read the nuggets of wisdom for what they are and then decide later, is it true, does it work, does it resonate with you? There are nuggets of wisdom you're about to learn that are not common knowledge. Some of this information you may already know and may have even heard many times before; however, you may know it intellectually, but it's not ingrained into your body and not integrated yet. So, if you see or feel any resistance or experience upset, it may be a part within you, that you aren't totally pleased with. This is where being compassionate with yourself and others comes into play.

So have fun, enjoy yourself, know your outcomes, set your intentions and the words will pop out. Your mind will be magnetically connected to this book.

I highly recommend you play full out, because you get what you put in. So if you put in 100%, you'll get back 100%, and if you only put out 10% then that's all you'll get. All the magic happens when you play full out doing the best you can with what you've got. The information you're about to learn has helped thousands and thousands of people worldwide and many of these truths span across cultures, nations and spiritual beliefs. The truth is the truth no matter what language it's in.

Let's get started...

Genius is making the complex simple. To take loads of information and distill it to nuggets of wisdom, so simple that a 5-year old can understand it. That's all it is. Over the course of this book, what you'll learn is that we're going simplify, giving you key action steps or key ingredients of the recipe for you to light up your world.

Information overload is one of the biggest challenges and problems we face. Right now, we have more information at our fingertips, with the Internet, than ever before in our lives. Yet, people are confused more than ever, because with a flood of more information it becomes more difficult to find out what the real valuable information is and cut out all the clutter of what's useless.

Design and Format of the Book

Design

We designed this book for you to easily consume and not become "Shelf Help". Most Chapters are about 10 pages long so you can read it all in one sitting or 1 chapter a day taking only 10-15 minutes of your time.

Format

Bio / Profile – For you to get to know the author.

Content – Authors sharing their wisdom.

Top 3 Takeaways and Action Steps – Summary to remember key points and action steps to create momentum and get results.

Free Gift from the author to go further and stay in touch.

EIJI MORISHITA

Bio:

Eiji "The Authority Genius" Morishita is CEO of Genius Squared and founder of the Genius Millionaire Academy. His mission is to create 1000 Millionaires to create movements that impact 1 Million people each. Eiji is passionate about empowering leaders to contribute their genius and stand out as the authority so that they can make a huge impact and create a lasting legacy. Eiji's genius is helping entrepreneurs and service professionals build profitable businesses offline without a business card or a website. Eiji and his businesses have been featured in LA & NY Times, CBC-TV Canada, and ABC World News Tonight. Previous clients include Palm, eBay, Sun Microsystems, and Nuance makers of Dragon Naturally Speaking.

Genius Profile

Name: Eiji Morishita
Biggest Challenge/Obstacle Overcome: Depression & Suicide

Top 3 Favorite Foods:
Mexican Food
Sushi
Regional BBQ (Texas, Memphis, Kansas City, St. Louis, Carolina)

Top 3 Favorite Musicians:
U2
AC/DC
Black Eyed Peas

Top 3 Favorite Places Visited:
1) Pebble Beach Golf Course, Monterey, CA
2) Kiyomizudera Temple, Kyoto, Japan
3) Costa Rica

Bucket List Item Not Yet Accomplished:
Playing Augusta National Golf Course

Top 3 Role Models or Heroes:
Jesus
Martin Luther King
Gandhi

Top 3 Takeaways to Slay the Genius Killers

1. Focus on Progress Not Perfection
Focusing on perfection kills your genius. Instead focus on what's going right and what could be improved.

2. Be Compassionate With Yourself and Others
Stop beating yourself up and killing your genius. It's like running in a marathon while beating yourself with a baseball bat. Life is a marathon, be good to yourself.

3. Do Only What You Are a Genius At, Delegate Non-Genius Activities
When you are inside your genius, it gives you energy and increases your confidence. When you unlock your genius and create your genius team, you become unstoppable and your results become inevitable.

Top 3 Action Steps

1. Schedule time in your calendar to read the book. Either block time out or commit to reading 1 chapter a day.
2. Perform the action steps written in each chapter.
3. Take advantage of the free gifts that our authors have generously given you.

Special Gift

Because you have purchased or received this book as a gift, you are gifted with 2 tickets, one for you and one for a friend to:

Unlock Your Genius Breakthrough Experience ($2590 Value)

During this groundbreaking, life-changing event, you will:

1. Discover your genius, define your uniqueness and design your message to share to the world.
2. Let go of what's been holding you back from the past.
3. Begin to live life on your terms and experience life with childlike enthusiasm, imagination, curiosity, and wonder.

CLAIM YOUR GIFT AT: www.GeniusSquared.com/pure-genius-gift

Use Code: **GENIUSBOOK** to receive your 2 complimentary tickets now.

FERLIE ALMONTE

BIO:

Exuberant.   Entertaining.   Magnetic. Mesmerizing. Hip. Holistic. RESILIENT.

There is no easy way to describe Ferlie Almonte. She is extraordinarily multi-talented, filled with wisdom and knowledge, and is a true beacon of light to many people seeking positive changes in their lives.

Ferlie Almonte is the CEO of Ferlilicious Enterprises, LLC. Her company provides Personal Transformation Products and Services. Under this enterprise, Ferlie is also the Designer and Creative Director of RESILIENCE by Ferlie Inspirational Jewelry and Apparel. Her mission to be the voice of hope, faith, courage and inspiration despite adversity propelled her to build Ferlilicious Enterprises.

Ferlie is no stranger to adversity. Born in the Philippines in 1962, She earned her Bachelors degree in Business Administration in 1982 and came to the US in 1984. Ferlie built a successful career in upscale retail sales management over 20 years, receiving awards and national recognition for her top sales performance. She took fashion design classes at FIT in NYC but switched to health care when she decided to have a family. Ferlie earned her certification as a Respiratory Therapist from Bergen Community College, while working full time. Disasters in life forced her to change jobs. Her marriage collapsed, the 9-11 disaster took her job, but the most devastating was her exposure to an occupational hazard that left her with permanent lung damage and severely debilitated for years. With hope and prayers, she received her miracle and went back to work. She reinvented her career. She landed a pharmaceutical sales position with Schering Plough. She also found love and got married. Her good fortune was short lived. She was laid off as a result of company merger, and lost her spouse to pancreatic cancer within eight months of marriage. Despite her string of misfortunes, Ferlie was always grateful, never resentful. RESILIENCE was her greatest gift. She decided to make an empowering choice to Turn her Mess into her Message and help people rise from their pain with grace and start over. Ferlie has advanced training and certification in Life Coaching from Coaching Cognition. She earned her Image Consulting certification from Image Resource Center in NY.

Ferlie co-authored an Amazon best selling book, Empowering Transformations for Women.

At her office at the Life and Image Transformation Center in Lodi, NJ, clients learn to Unleash their B.L.I.N.G. (Boldly Living in Natural Greatness) and begin their journey to an empowered, joyful, meaningful and authentic life.

For more information, please visit www.UnleashyourBling.com or send an email to info@ResiliencebyFerlie.com

GENIUS PROFILE:

Name: Ferlinda "Ferlie" Almonte
Biggest Challenge/Obstacle Overcome:

One only? Are you kidding me? I AM A SURVIVOR EXTRAORDINAIRE. I have mastered Resilience from the multitude of adversities I've risen from with grace and swagger!

(Abandonment, Poverty, Debilitating illness, Loss of Spouse to Pancreatic cancer as a newlywed, loss of mother to ovarian cancer, loss of father to lung cancer, a horrible divorce, abusive relationships, a string of job lay offs,

financial hardship, loss of home, and being gay (never had issues really with my sexuality really, but to others, it is an adversity).
I have successfully turned every single Mess into my Message!

Top 3 Favorite Foods:
DESSERTS (and FRUITS especially mango…Mango tarts),
LENGUA (Ox tongue)
SHRIMPS….Oh my!!! I'm hungry now!

Top 3 Favorite Musicians:
Andrea Bocelli…his voice pierces my soul
Celine Dion…there's passion in every note to her songs
Myself …I love my versatility and how I make messages of the songs come alive

Top 3 Favorite Places Visited:
Laguna Beach,
Niagara Falls,
Universal Studios

(I was in awe of the magnificence of nature and how it speaks to me. Universal Studios stimulates the mind on what can be possible and allows the spirit to experience the possibilities the mind and humans can create.

Nature invites you to dream and imagine what you can be, it reminds us of the innate beauty within us. Universal Studios shows us the many possibilities we can be when we put our talents into passion filled careers in many forms of arts and technology ,and bring joy and entertainment to millions.

Bucket List Item Not Yet Accomplished:
Never been to Europe. I would love to go on a Mediterranean Cruise

Top 3 Role Models or Heroes:
My Mother.~ Epitome of beauty, strength, grace, class, integrity and character.
Oprah. ~ Biggest lesson in living our best lives.
Ellen Degeneres~ Inspiration on being true to oneself, authenticity and generosity at its finest.

MAKING YOUR MESS YOUR MESSAGE

Discovering your Own Genius after Life Devastation

by Ferlinda "Ferlie" Almonte

"It is not the strongest of the species that survives, nor the most intelligent that survives. It is the one that is the most adaptable to change."
Charles Darwin

Eiji Morishita defined genius as a level of performance that is beyond the ordinary, a unique gift and a powerful message that the world desperately needs to hear.

It was a relief to find out that the fantastic intention of this book is not based on the context of IQ, but is focused on sharing our mastery in a subject matter that is relevant and important to empower ordinary people into unleashing their extraordinary possibilities, through our messages.

Unlike many authorities on different fields of expertise, specialized education and training on resilience is not obtained from a traditional university. A graduate credit is not earned with every blow in life you overcome. Your classroom is the world you live in. You meet your teachers as you live through the many colorful chapters of your life. You will learn and sharpen your life skills through your own, unique transformational experiences. Your lessons will not be delivered to you packaged with a bow. Many of them will come as a blow. Some will take you to the deepest dark and leave you wondering if you want to continue or drop out of your scary journey. Your decision will determine your future. You will undergo a spiritual strength training when you choose to keep pressing forward and work through your resistance.

Your credentials will be ingrained in your soul in the valuable life lessons you learned. And what you earn is not just knowledge, but wisdom. The kind of person you become is your diploma. The difference is remarkable.

WHO YOU BECOME IS A PUBLIC BROADCAST OF YOUR CHOICES IN LIFE. You get to choose to be an inspiration or a lesson to others.

Funny how I found myself often saying, "I feel like I have a PhD from the University of Adversity," never imagining that one day I will be invited to write about my journey in discovering my genius on resilience. First, I said "WHOA!!! I have no degree or training on that", and doubted if I was the right person to do the job. After my brief moment of uncertainty, I took a deep breath, silenced the noises and distractions in my head, and reflected. In my stillness, I heard the voice within me! I have been training ALL MY LIFE for this moment. To share the wisdom I have earned from the multiple and repeated blows, challenges, tragedies and adversities I've had since childhood. I rose above each one of those devastations with grace, dignity, courage and boldness in my soul to start over again. I am living in my zones of genius, joy and serenity because I fully embraced the scary and audacious choices I made, claimed my chances for new beginnings with no guarantees, lived a charged life, and learned to trust my angels to watch over me. People can learn from my experiences, and be assured, that just like me, they can find hope in their horizon, that they can be happy again, that they will not just survive, but thrive, even after our spirits have been paralyzed from the tragic losses of our loved ones, after being dumped, laid off, being severely ill or simply feeling invisible in a crowd for so long. I said to myself, it will be a big disservice to others who need to hear my message if don't share my story and my genius. That was the moment when I realized that I achieved the status of PhD ~ Past having Doubts. Ha! I just caught myself shifting from limiting to empowering mindset. Being mindful of the quality of our thoughts is crucial to our ability to adapt and rise to the challenges of life. They need to serve our purpose and the higher good. Our thoughts do become our realities. We often talk ourselves out of our own healing, solutions and our own progress through negative self talk. Every now and then, we slip into self-doubt. Self-awareness makes us realize its value to ourselves and to others. That self-awareness led me to confidently step into my genius and share how resilience led me to my brilliance.

As I take you through my heart wrenching story in this chapter, you will understand how I stepped into the magnificent level of genius on resilience that God intended for me to be. I was put through 50 years of adversity boot camp. It got me thinking that God made sure I go through what seems to be the most ridiculous and rigorous training someone can endure. God made me extraordinarily tough in spirit and tested my limits. I passed with flying colors. It was also through my tsunami of misfortunes that I discovered my mission in life.

To quote Mark Twain, "There are two important days in someone's life…the day we were born, and the day we find out why." It took me 50 years to find my why, and when I did, I felt reborn. I felt like a new person. Divine empowerment seemed to have seeped into my veins, and every cell of my body was infused with a potent mission…To be the Voice of Hope, Faith, Courage and Inspiration despite Adversity, and to be The Teacher of Resilience.

 I talked to God and said, "Lord, I now understand why you've put me through so much more tests than I thought was humanly possible to endure. You made me experience everything I've been through so I can learn to listen with my heart, to hear the voices of those hurting when words quit on them, to guide with compassion, to teach with wisdom and understanding, and to help people rise from the depth of their sorrows and pain. I think I have enough material now." Yes, I actually added a little humor into my plea to God to now give me a break. I thanked God for my precious lessons, and never asked, "Why me?" I believe with all my heart that he chose me because He knew I had the will not to allow myself to be defeated.

Every person has a story. Most of us have experienced some form of hardship, heartache or pain that somehow shook our world, crushed us, pushed us to the tipping point of our sanity, opened our minds to new perspectives, awakened our souls, changed our hearts, and shaped us to kind of persons we are now. The difference in who we become is how well we adapt and bounce back during those moments when we get blindsided and knocked down from our perfectly planned dreams, by horrific, life changing catastrophes we never imagined could happen to us.

I certainly had my hefty share of adversities in life. With no exaggeration, my life story has enough juicy details, drama, conflict and exhilarating twists, not just for a book, but for a movie trilogy. I grew up without a father. My faithful and devoted mother raised us, four children, with the help of relatives. I have experienced poverty. I've had abusive relationships, and a nasty, costly divorce. I had a string of job layoffs from lucrative paying positions. I have felt the excruciating pain of losing my precious mother to ovarian cancer within three months of diagnosis, and lost my father six months after, to lung cancer. Both of my parents were 58 years young. The pivotal moment of my life took place when I suffered from a severely debilitating occupational hazard injury that left me with a permanent lung damage, struggling to breathe and unable to work for years. I would, literally, turn blue merely walking a short distance of two feet. I was numb and speechless when my pulmonologist said to me these dreaded words,"I do not want to scare you, but this concerns me. Your airways and vagus nerve are hyper reactive and will act on their own once triggered. No amount of medication or inhaler can save you once the vagus nerve is triggered." In words I could not remember exactly, he managed to tell me that I could die at any time. It was then that I learned to live my life as though each day is my last. My Harvard trained doctor did not give up on me. He sent me to a neurologist with hopes of finding a way to control the hyper- reactivity of my vagus nerve. The neurologist found a drug that calmed that nerve and helped manage my airways more effectively. However, I noticed that I was going blind from the side effects of the drug that helped me breathe. Oh no!!! I wanted to be alive for my daughter, but asked myself if a blind mother would be any use to her. Will I just be a burden? I can't remember praying as fervently as I did in my life…praying hard for healing. I got my miracle. I got my second chance at life AND in love. I was deliriously happy to find and marry my true love. But my happiness was short lived. I tragically lost my spouse to pancreatic cancer within eight months of marriage, three months after being diagnosed. My world crumbled. At about the same time, I was laid off from my pharmaceutical sales position, which led to extreme financial hardship. I lost the very first house I bought on my own.

Yes, I've gone through all that. I probably had many valid excuses to whine, complain and indulge in self pity. But I chose not to. I MADE A DECISION TO TURN MY MESS INTO MY MESSAGE.

During those moments when I was down on my luck, I WAS ALWAYS GRATEFUL, NEVER RESENTFUL. It was unbelievably hard to remain in a place of gratitude when times were challenging. But never losing sight of counting our blessings in the midst of our difficulties somehow makes our load feel lighter. I always believed in messages concealed in adversities. Before my spouse succumbed to the inevitable, a surgeon sat next to me and shared a beautiful verse from the bible. He read to me, (Jeremiah 29) [11]"For I know the plans I have for you," declares the Lord, "plans to prosper you and not to harm you, plans to give you hope and a future." I found comfort, hope and empowerment on those words, and kept the message safely tucked in my heart to this day.

What is your story? What do your scars tell you? What made you feel so bitter and resentful? Who left your heart cut wide open to bleed? Why do you feel invisible, undesirable and unappreciated? Who took away your dreams and confidence? How long do you intend to remain confined within the walls of your pain and fears?

Tragedies in life can leave us paralyzed and unable to get back up. Sometimes, when a loved one dies, a part of us dies with them and we lose the ability to live alone. There are also times when the one we chose to grow old with, makes us feel just as alone, in their presence. The difference does not seem much, dead or alive. How many people do you know were practically married to their careers, devoting their time and energy to work, sacrificing moments with their loved ones, only to feel so dispensable and worthless when the company they practically gave their lives to, decide to downsize and let them go? Welcome to your new reality! You can either fight your reality like an oak and snap in the middle of a storm, or be a willow that follows the direction of the wind and survive in one piece. Adaptability is Survivability. You can stay angry, stubborn and stressed out, but your situation will remain the same. Or you can choose to be open and go with the flow and strive to discover exciting new opportunities that will manifest in your lives. The circumstances of my adversities forced me to reinvent. Life is a constant evolution. Resilience is a must to survive. I would not be writing this chapter if I chose to fight lost battles.

How do we move on? How do we heal? There is no magic pill.
People heal differently. Some people need professional help in the process. Others don't, but need to be inspired and guided through the transition.

Life has taught me that we need give ourselves permission to grieve any loss, and to grant ourselves time to find a comfortable place within our souls to cope better and begin to heal. When someone we love passes on, the ache of our loss does not go away, but we are able to deal with the pain a little easier over time. We never stop loving our departed loved ones. We keep them in a sacred place in our hearts. The reality of life is that we are still here. We can choose to be crippled perpetually by our tragedy, or we can honor their memory and keep the love we share with them alive by breathing life, joy and meaning into our tomorrows. How we choose to continue our earthly journey is a wonderful tribute to them.

Forgiveness is crucial to healing. When we learn to forgive those who have wronged us, and learn to forgive ourselves for having allowed our pain to continue to have the power to hurt us, healing takes place. Getting rid of that baggage that weighs us down and keeps us unable to soar brings freedom and profound peace and happiness.

Stop the blame game. No one wins in that game. Our ego oftentimes blocks us from being happy. Our attitude can make or break us. Let go of what cannot be undone and what we cannot control. Shifting our perspective makes a huge difference in our serenity. By also empowering ourselves with positive thoughts and energy, our fighting chance and the possibility to transition into the promising new chapters of our lives becomes more achievable. **Grieve, forgive, and receive.**

Do not allow the guilt of moving on hold you back. The fear of judgment that people will not be as sympathetic as we bounce back keeps us stuck. We sometimes feel that playing a victim seems more comfortable. People are kinder. But, how does that serve your goals and your future? Do we play dead while we are still alive for a little attention? Do you keep yourself stagnant to gain the approval of those who would rather see you rot in your misery?
You are worthy and deserving to be happy again.

Resilience involves learning to choose your battles. Resilience is your ability to adapt through life's setbacks and hardships. It is something we develop by learning to adapt to difficulties and failures, and allows us to develop self-management skills from the wisdom we learn from our experiences. A resilient person remains tough, hopeful, positive, flexible, able to recover and accept life's new realities, after coming face to face with devastation. "Strong people alone know how to organize their suffering so as to bear only the most necessary pain."

Emil Dorian

Reinventions and transformations begin with a decision that you are ready and willing to do what it takes to change your state of being and your future. That decision can be reached by having clarity on the quality of life you want for the rest of your life. Our soul has the innate ability to repair itself when damaged, becoming stronger than ever. It is our minds, sometimes, that is non-compliant.

There is no shame in failing. We cannot continue to live our lives protected by walls we built to shield ourselves from getting hurt, falling short or failing miserably. There is no shame in giving it your best shot and missing the goal. The ball can't get to the goal if you keep your arms tightly wrapped around it. You need to release your dream, put your heart in it, and pray hard.

Release yourself from the captivity of your self- imposed limitations and fears.

AUDACITY BREEDS PROSPERITY. Getting back up after life knocked you down is not easy. But YOU ARE WORTH A BRAND NEW START. Underneath your mess lies your message. Find it. ALLOW RESILIENCE TO UNLOCK YOUR BRILLIANCE. Muster the courage to step into your light. BE AUDACIOUS! Follow your bliss! Unleash your B.L.I.N.G.! Stand out and Sparkle in your B.L.I.N.G.! Boldly Living In Natural Greatness is a spectacular way to make a fresh start. The scars of your past are there to remind you of where you've been, but do not have to define where you are going. Your future is filled with amazing possibilities. The door to your best life is wide open. You simply need to walk through it to embrace the magnificent life that awaits you. What is stopping you now?

"Healing would not take place if we continue to reside in the past. When we step fully into the present and open our hearts to new beginnings, the magic of healing, spiritual resurrection and emotional rejuvenation takes place ."

Ferlie Almonte

QUICK ACTION STEPS:

DECIDE TO TURN YOUR LIFE FROM MISERABLE TO INVINCIBLE

ADJUST YOUR ATTITUDE. Determine what you can, and cannot control. Change it or Suck it up! (or use Deal with it)

SILENCE THE NOISES IN YOUR HEAD and FOLLOW YOUR HEART

SURROUND YOURSELF WITH PEOPLE WHO WILL ELEVATE YOU TO BE RESILIENT AND BE BRILLIANT!.

Special Gift

RESILIENCE TO BRILLIANCE
   Momentum Package
Visit www.UnleashyourBling.com and
Enjoy your FREE MP3 DownLoad on
   Ferlilicious and Delicious Food for the Soul
Inspirational Tips on How to feel Sexy,Epic and Alive Again
After Tragedies

Get an exclusive 25% discount on all the unique and fabulous
RESILIENCE by Ferlie Inspirational Jewelry & Apparel
Visit www.ResiliencebyFerlie.com, shop and enjoy the 25%
discount by entering the promo code GENIUS at checkout.

Experience an Unforgettable 20 Minute COMPLIMENTARY
Ferlilicious Discover your B.L.I.N.G. Session
Spots are very limited. Find out how you can Boldly Live In
Natural Greatness
Book an appointment by sending an email to info@
ResiliencebyFerlie.com

DIANE CASTELL

BIO:

In the 45 plus years that Diane has been working in financial services she has always had a thirst for knowing why and how things are done. This thirst has led her to study in many areas over the course of her life and learn new ways of thinking and acting when it comes to relationships, styles of dressing, beliefs, the effect of language in her life and the importance of finances.

The current chapter of Diane's life has seen her as a single mother to eight, yes that's right I said eight, children that are only 10 years apart in age. This is where the rubber really hit the road. With all of these children and a burning desire to educate them, while being an example, in other ways to think and understand different perspectives she has attended seminars about Kinesiology, homeopathic remedies, business and more.

As she was raising her children Diane created her own financial services practice. Her desire to stay home with her children and make a living made this an easy choice. She finished her accounting degree just before the birth of her 3rd child and since then has gone on to complete other certifications in Feng Shui, Reiki, Essential Oil training, Touch for Health and more.

Throughout her years she has worked a number of jobs in addition owning her own business where she worked with a wide variety of small business owners and had the opportunity to see many different ways that businesses can work as well as identifying some ways that do not work.

GENIUS PROFILE:

Name: Diane Castell

Biggest Challenge/Obstacle Overcome: Moving forward from a marriage that was not working even though I was 3 months pregnant with my 8th child and had 7 other children 10 and under.

Top 3 Favorite Foods:
    Brussel Sprouts
    Beets
    Broccoli

Top 3 Favorite Musicians:
    Chicago
    Peter Cetera
    Rascal Flatts

Top 3 Favorite Places Visited:
    Mount Rushmore
    Washington DC
    Hawaii

Bucket List Item Not Yet Accomplished:
    Travel to China
    Moscow
    Thailand with my children

Top 3 Role Models or Heroes:
    David Neagle
    Tom Hanks
    Sidney Poitier

LIVING LIFE FROM QUESTIONING THE NORM

by Diane Castell

When she was 3 months pregnant with her eighth child, Michelle was faced with some challenging decisions. Her marriage of eleven years was less than ideal and another round of promises her husband had made were being broken rapidly. Throughout their marriage he would tell her stories or make promises and she would find out they were exaggerations or lies. This caused a conflict for her because she did not want her children to grow up believing that this was acceptable behavior and on the other side her mother consistently taught her that if there was a problem in the relationship she needed to do something to make it work.

Finally Michelle decided the time had come to get a divorce. She called her parents and asked them to come help her get herself and the children back home. Her parents agreed to come and they made the arrangements to come.

It was not easy for her to leave, she was concerned about her children growing up without a father figure, but by this time she knew that her then husband did not really care about the children. She also knew that she would have to provide for them. Thankfully her father had his own business which she had worked in for many years so he gave her a job and a place to live.

The time came for the baby to be born and Michelle went to the hospital. The doctor was a friend and knew the situation. Before the delivery though he asked, "Is anyone coming?", "No", said Michelle, "There is not anyone to come". The reason was that her mother was taking care of the other children and her father did not handle these types of situations well, he would not be able to provide any comfort. The doctor was really nice and stayed with her as much as possible to make the situation easier.

Michelle continued to live with her parents for awhile and then the opportunity presented itself for her to move back into her house, it had been rented out; she was scared because she knew she would be the only adult the house. On the other side she was excited because she was tired of hearing her father complain about small things the children would do that he did not like. She learned from hearing him complain about her son, who the moment he was inside the house would take off his shoes, or her daughter that did not cook her toast as dark as he thought she should. She learned you need to decide which things are really important to make an issue over and which are not, or people will remember you as someone who is constantly upset. The other piece is to set boundaries, make sure that the boundary is important and non-negotiable otherwise it is not really a boundary. In her applying this Michelle found that it brought her respect, her children and other people knew they could rely on what she said, they may not like it but they could believe that what she said she meant.

After she had moved into her own house Michelle found she really enjoyed the freedom from the criticism that she had known for a long time growing up. She decided she needed to learn more about how to create better relationships because whatever we saw our parents do is also how we tend to handle various situations. She wanted to create something better and realized it would take some concerted effort. One of the first things she learned about was thanking her children for making their beds or cleaning their rooms. Her first thought was, " Why should I thank them for doing things like that? They should do those things anyway." She realized that this was her father's attitude and so she decided to try it. The amazing part to her was once she started thanking her children for doing chores, no matter the size, they were more willing to do more chores and they would do a better job. This was great! People really respond to praise and are willing to do more once they have received some positive recognition.

Another aspect that Michelle wanted to understand better were was to keep her children healthy without giving them prescription drugs. She had seen her mother have adverse reactions to prescription drugs along with a friend who almost died due to taking common prescription drugs. Michelle knew that there had to be alternatives that were safer and without the side effects. A trusted friend introduced her to essential oils. She read about them and tried oils from many different companies and finally settled on one company where the oils consistently delivered results and the continuing education was excellent. This really helped because when her children would get ear aches or stomach aches she could put an oil on them and they would be recover quickly. Another aspect that she liked was even if she used the wrong oil, it would not harm them or herself in any way. One year when there was a large number of cases of bronchitis where she lived, a friend came to her and was complaining about how many times she had been to the doctor and how many rounds of antibiotics she had taken and that she still had bronchitis. Michelle told her that bronchitis was due to a virus and antibiotics would not kill a virus. She gave her friend an oil and in a few days the friend called to thank her, she was finally over the bronchitis.

Michelle realized that the more she learned, the more she wanted to learn, understand and implement. She continued to study and eventually came across Touch for Health. Touch for Health is a way to bring the body back into balance through kinesiology. This excited Michelle as a way to be able to create lasting change and bring that body into balance.

Our bodies are all like automatic thermostats. If we are uncomfortable with a change in our lives it throws our bodies out of balance, just like a thermostat the system kicks on to keep us where we are comfortable, through kinesiology (muscle testing) we can fix the imbalance and make the change easier.   Michelle incorporated this into her life and was amazed at the results. Through kinesiology you can easily test if you have an allergy or a food intolerance to a particular food. You can also test to see if a food or supplement would be beneficial for you. This has helped her tremendously in keeping her children healthy. Even before this Michelle studied more nutritious ways to eat. She had always liked vegetables growing up and now she learned more the benefits from each vegetable and more ways to fix them. In dealing with her now former husband by just making a few changes to his diet he had fewer moods swings and was less depressed. The first time his mother came to visit after they had been married a while she asked what Michelle had done to create this change in him. The biggest difference was his diet; less meat, no soda pop (which he really liked), drinking water, less sugar and more vegetables.

Another aspect that became apparent to Michelle was the importance of language. Language affects the way we feel and also the way people react to us. One of the most interesting aspects that she learned was that when you say something derogatory about another person, your subconscious takes it that you are saying this about yourself. By being more positive in our language patterns and self talk, we have the ability to change our moods quickly and change the moods of others around us. When you walk into a situation that you have played out in your mind, it is more likely to occur just the way you played it out in your mind. Part of that is the energy we create around ourselves due to the self talk and then we walk into the situation with an expectation. When we are looking for a situation to turn out a certain way our mind deletes, distorts and generalizes to confirm our beliefs. Michelle found that in teaching this to her children, others and utilizing it herself how many situations changed and became more positive.

Now that many basics were taken care of Michelle decided to study Feng Shui and became certified in it. Through this she found that by adding color to your environment and rearranging your furniture it created better feelings in your home and added a richness that was not there before. All the houses she had previously lived in her mother insisted that they be painted white. When she began to paint her home in more bold colors her mother was shocked, but the more her mother came over she really liked the change.

Then the opportunity came along for learning colors and styles that suited her more. This experience was amazing because Michelle felt like her clothes, in style and color, supported her personality more. Once she changed the style and colors she was wearing the number of compliments she received from other people skyrocketed, and even her own children told her that she seemed nicer now. By dressing in the colors and styled that complimented her skin tone and her personality she came across as a warmer and more authentic person, like she was always meant to.

Michelle continues to learn, grow and change because one of her goals is to create a positive impact on the world. She now understands more and more how important your beliefs are and that many of them came from other people. When it came to her religious views, relationship skills and more she realized that they mostly came from her parents. When she began to question these beliefs and look at them from a different perspective she realized that many of them really did not produce the results that she was looking for and how important it was to change them. She stills falls back into old patterns, but now she recognizes the patterns more quickly and makes changes to them faster and easier.

There is still more to come as she continues to study and learn each and every day.

Steps to creating better relationships.

1. Sincerely compliment and thank people for what they do well.
2. Tell important people in your life that you love them every day. Hug them, kiss them, and create fond memories with them.
3. Take care of little problems while they are little to dissolve tension before it builds and becomes a crisis.

Steps to creating better health.

1. Drink at least half of your body weight in ounces everyday in water. Plain water (lemons are welcome).
2. Read labels on anything you buy. If it looks like a science experiment or has ingredients that you do not recognize or cannot pronounce, don't buy it.
3. Eat more vegetables. Learn how to fix them, it really helps.

Special Gift

Gift: Go to www.zealovation.com to choose between a free financial tracker, free health tracker or a free improved relationship tracker.

Gift 2: a reduced price ticket to the Zealovation event in September. Regular price of the ticket is $797 your special price is $297 use the code Ilivewithzeal13.

LINDA CRAWFORD

BIO:

Linda Crawford is a California Cuisine Gourmet Cook and a Gluten/Allergen/Toxin Specialist who offers coaching and consulting regarding gluten-free eating, food allergen symptoms relief and chemical toxin reduction.

Linda received her Bachelors degree in Business and Nutrition in 1995 then started her first business as a Nutritional Counselor – educating clients about balancing meals, metabolism, and eating habits. She now offers tips on organic shopping, reducing toxins in the body, home and personal care products. She works with clients to understand ingredient labeling and kitchen-pantry makeovers. She conducts home cooking parties, cooking demos and menu planning to help her clients uncover disguised sugar, carbs and chemical toxin ingredients in everyday products consumed. For more information about her coaching and consulting services, checkout her website at: www.LifestyleChanges2Health.com

For more information on her home cooking parties, GF-AF recipes and personal chef home parties, checkout her website at: www.PleasinThePalate.com. Linda is currently working on a Gluten, Allergy-free, and healthy eating e-cookbook targeted to be released in 2014.

GENIUS PROFILE:

Name: Linda S. Crawford

Biggest Challenge/Obstacle Overcome: Reactions to gluten/food intolerances (Wheat, corn, soy, peanuts, casein in milk) for the last (9) years. This is why I became a Health coach specializing in gluten, food allergies and chemical toxins.

Top 3 Favorite Foods:
Dark chocolate
Seafood
Fresh organic produce

Top 3 Favorite Musicians:
Rascal Flatts
Wayman Tisdale
B.B .King

Top 3 Favorite Places Visited:
South Caribbean
Lake Tahoe
Austria

Bucket List Item Not Yet Accomplished:

Stay on an Italian farm and shop, prepare and cook meals with a local Italian chef using local produce, pasta, meats and wines. They don't allow GMO foods in Italy!

Top 3 Role Models or Heroes:
Jacque Cousteau
My Grandmother
Deepak Chopra

CREATING SIMPLE SOLUTIONS THAT WORK

by LINDA CRAWFORD

Natural Cleanse by Eliminating Reactive Foods You Eat

Importance of healthy eating to nourish the body

People are in shock when I tell them that a 100-calorie "healthy" food like green beans or oatmeal can cause a two-pound weight gain, increase the aging process and heighten health issues. How does this happen? The simplest answer is inflammatory response and how these foods react with your body chemistry. But what exactly does that mean and how can you be so affected by a healthy food?

Many systems come into play with a reactive food and this causes the domino effect that we usually associate with getting older – think expanding waistline, declining energy or health.

Even though we are living longer, we are not living healthier.

Let's start with some basics. Poor nutrition can be due to eating nutritionally depleted foods like refined and processed foods and/or poor absorption of nutrients due to intestinal issues. Also, aging is a state of inflammation. So as we age, digestive enzyme production slows down. We start to produce less stomach acid and saliva all of which aid digestion. The foods we used to be able to break down easily when we were younger become more difficult to digest. These foods have now become trigger foods and sensitivities and affect multiple systems that alter weight and health.

Declining thyroid function as another example of how aging and foods can affect your weight. The thyroid is responsible for many functions including metabolism, sex drive, skin, hair and energy levels. Hormones become unbalanced as we age and this affects the thyroid. A standard "healthy" diet will include foods known as goitrogens and these foods attack the thyroid. Some examples of goitrogens are spinach, arugula, cauliflower and strawberries.

Thyroid Dysfunction

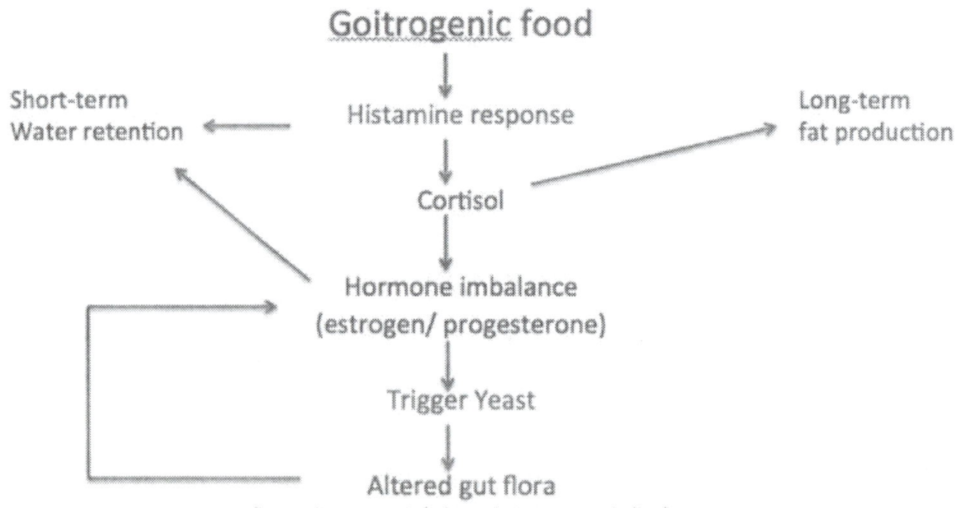

Food sensitivity is also an example of how weight and health are triggered by a reactive food. Histamine, an important part of our immune system, is automatically triggered when an inflammatory food is introduced. Histamine causes immediate water retention by causing capillaries to dilate and allowing them to leak fluid.

To control this histamine response, the body produces cortisol. Cortisol and hormones such as progesterone and testosterone use the same building blocks; the more cortisol that is released, the more your hormonal balance is negatively affected. The body is producing cortisol at the expense of progesterone and testosterone. These hormonal fluctuations disrupt water balance, metabolism, thyroid health, healthy sex drive and immune response. Elevated cortisol produces glucose which leads to increased blood sugar levels. This will start to affect yeast growth, altered gut flora, and could be a reason behind the incredible rise of type 2 diabetes in the US. Altered gut flora leads to a weakened immune response as the balance of our intestinal bacteria is thrown off. Remember that 80% of our immune system is in our guts!

Food Sensitivity

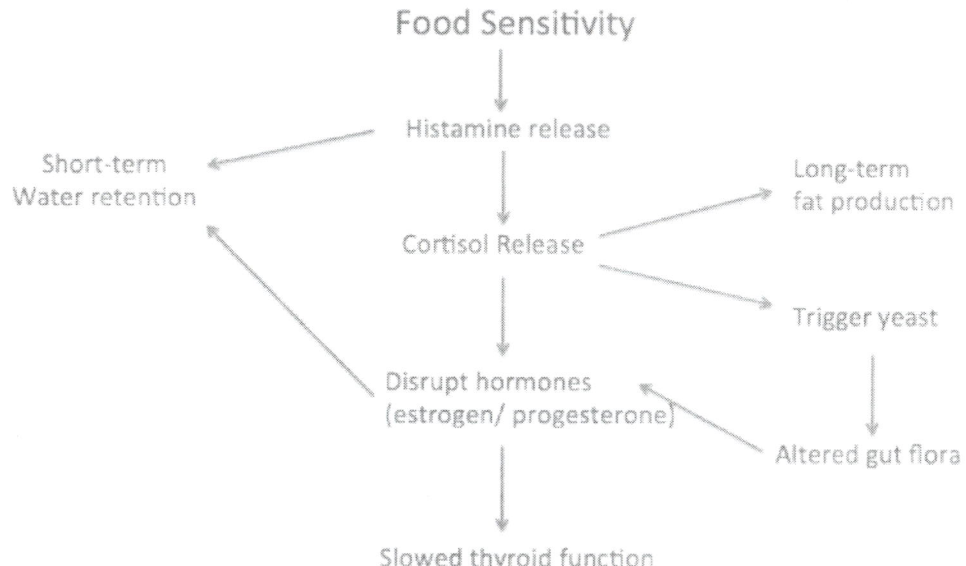

Can all of this happen from just a cup of green beans? Absolutely! In addition, this inflammatory response can easily last 72 hours. So, just a few "healthy" foods a week can cause that scale to go up year after year no matter how many calories you count and how much you exercise!

The 3-Day Cleanse

How do you find your reactive foods? By doing a safe, food-based cleanse with the least reactive foods and then slowly reintroducing the foods YOU love. This cleanse is a method that allows you to systematically test foods and know which foods work for your unique chemistry. You will discover which foods make you feel vital, healthy, full of energy and lean. The most amazing part of discovering *your* healthy foods is rediscovering the body's amazing ability to self-heal and how rapidly you can lose weight.

Some of the most reactive foods are the following, ironically considered to be some of the top health foods by most:

- Turkey
- Oatmeal
- Greek yogurt
- Black beans
- Salmon
- Asparagus
- Cauliflower
- Farm raised fish
- Deli meats

Sushi (usually not high quality fish)

This 3-day cleanse contains a daily average of 2,200 calories for women and an average of 2,800 calories for men. The average weight loss is 5-8 lbs. How is that possible? You will quickly learn on this cleanse program that the calorie myth means nothing – all that matters is how easily your body can digest foods. The "cleaner" your foods are, the more food you can eat and the better you feel.

The steps leading up to this three-day cleanse are very easy:

- First thing in the morning, drink 16 ounces of water with lemon, preferably warm.
- Have dandelion tea with breakfast. The tea and the lemon are wonderful natural liver cleansers and will aid metabolism and hormonal health.
- Take a probiotic (50 Billion live cultures) each morning with breakfast to restore digestive health.
- Drink 6-8 glasses of water each day by 8PM.
- Cut "white foods" from your daily regimen: potatoes, sugar, rice, breads and pasta

It's very important that you do not deviate from the cleanse; the days are structured to have adequate nutrients, protein, fat and fiber to keep you full. In fact, the first day for women on this cleanse program has you consuming 70-plus grams of vegetarian protein and over 100% of your macronutrients and minerals.

What is in it for you?

This cleanse program allows you to eat the least reactive foods during the first three days. These foods are easily digestible and your body gets a rest from breaking down inflammatory foods. Energy is diverted from difficult digestion to repair. Systems that were first affected by reactive foods show immediate improvement – stress levels, hormones, skin, and digestion all rapidly improve.

In the first few days after the cleanse, you can introduce foods that are lower reactive, such as cheese, steak, wheat and wine. Your body will quickly let you know in many ways whether these new foods work for you. Weight response to a new food is a gauge, but so are sleep, mood, stress levels and digestion to name just a few.

Are there any side effects?

I have devised this cleanse to be as easy as possible, but there is the possibility that the release of toxins can cause some discomfort. It is better to deal with this now (really!) than later on when disease starts to crop up in a more serious form.

If you do start to feel a cleanse reaction such as a headache or nausea, double-strength peppermint tea will often make symptoms subside. If aspirin is part of your protocol, then please feel free to take one if you feel a headache coming on. Suffering will not help on many levels; there is no need to "tough it out." Think of these three days as the most important investment – your path back to vibrant health and a healthy weight, based on your body structure.

How will it make my life easier?

Here are (3) takeaways that will improve your waistline:

- Your body's reaction to certain foods will decrease because you will now know which foods do not work well within your digestive system.
- Inflammation in your gut will heal which means you will begin to fully nourish your body with less reactive foods and gain full nutrient benefit at the cellular level.
- Fatigue/Low Energy will subside and you will regain your vitality because you are feeding your body at the cellular level.

Managing your reactions at the digestive system level that will allow you to live a healthy lifestyle versus reacting to symptoms brought on by gluten, chemical toxins, and other food allergies. So sign up for my free gifts to receive more details on this 3 day Cleanse. Having your health restored will give you the ability to work smart, function at a high energy level and live a long, healthy, vibrant lifestyle.

Special Gift

My Free Gifts to You

An exploratory breakthrough for a 30 minute follow-up session to check-in, to ask any questions you need answers for to determine any road blocks keeping you from your weight goal towards optimum health. This will be offered to the first (20) readers who contact me to at: www.LifestyleChanges2Health.com Just enter "Genius" in the subject line when you sign up for the (2) gifts on the homepage. ($150 value)

Full listing of Reactive Foods for 2013 categorized by the (%) of reaction in the body.($30 value)

3 day cleanse food chart, supplements and shopping list to guide you through 3 days. ($30 value)

DIANA DENTINGER

BIO:

Diana Dentinger is a Personality Expert and Corporate Team Building Specialist.

She is known for her insightful and untraditional tools that captivate CEOs and employees. They learn from her how to engage wholeheartedly to stay in the company game or she sparks their entre-preneurial spirit so they get out.

She is a game changer for every company she has served by catalyzing new ways to show up at work and in the world. Her clients are from the Automotive industry, Local and Regional Government, the Public Sector and Production.

After noticing an overall dissatisfaction with old style personality question-naires and assessements, she created a more wholistic one to meet the needs of today's busy yet profound people. It is the easiest, most exact and effective tool on the market. It has helped hundreds of professionals over the past years increase their self confidence, double their performance, save time and money.

She combined her research on human programming, essential human needs and ancient wisdom then put it into a fun format. Her clients are coached down an unexplored path to tap into their personal potential. They say "It is amazing". She travels the world over to host personal growth workshops.

Diana has lived and worked in Europe since 1984 raising her 4 children in Italy. Intrigued by the resourcefulness in the "out of the box" younger generations she committed to improve how to raise children, how to communicate in the family and how to live a happy life. Monthly she connects with thousands of parents through her digital magazine to raise consciousness worldwide.

She is a neurobiology therapist, published author, magazine editor and international speaker. Visit her at: www.dianadentinger.com or contact her for training and coaching at: diana@dianadentinger.com

GENIUS PROFILE:

Name: Diana Dentinger
Biggest Challenge/Obstacle Overcome:
Having to sleep!
Not having teletransportation to be where I want to be in an instant!

Top 3 Favorite Foods:
Spaghetti with lobster,
Lasagna with pesto,
Gelato al gianduja (creamy nutella flavored ice cream!)

Top 3 Favorite Musicians:
Diana Ross and the supremes (obvious for our name!)
Whitney Houston – for the words in her song
"The Greatest Love"
I believe the children are our future / Teach them well and let them lead the way / Show them all the beauty they possess inside / Give them a sense of pride"
Michael Jackson – since I grew up with "Abc, 123" and I love to dance

Top 3 Favorite Places Visited:
Venice Italy for the romantic atmosphere
Sao Jorge Brazil for the energy in the national park filled with crystals!
New Zealand for an experience with the Maori tribe

Bucket List Item Not Yet Accomplished:
Have an experience living with the Aborigines in Australia.
Learn the American native tribal connections with nature, plants and animals.
Rent a castle to host a family reunion in Italy with my 200 relatives.

Top 3 Role Models or Heroes:
I have had such powerful members in my family:
Grandmothers who were very feminine, filled with a profound faith, loving to their 9 children and supportive to their husbands and never too tired to help;
Grandfathers who were ethical, disciplined and hard -working men.
A few friends who were always happy, smiley and appreciative throughout their illnesses until the end of their physical experience.

THE 22 INNATE NEEDS WHAT IS REALLY DRIVING YOU!

by **Diana Dentinger**

"Know yourself and you will know the universe and the gods."
Engraving on the front of the Oracle of Apollo Temple, Delphi Greece

"Why can't you just sit still?" "What are you being so picky about?" "Are you a control freak?" "Why are you always preaching me?" "When will you ever relax?" "Aren't you ever going to stay home?" "Why don't you say something?"

Have observations like these ever been directed at you? How did you answer back?

If you are like the majority of people, you started justifying your behavior and making up excuses for why you were doing what you were doing. You felt judged or misunderstood. Maybe you lashed out to defend your actions or just gave into the other person and even felt wrong doing what you were doing.

This chapter is all about creating a new experience for you. It's about seeing what you do and why from a whole new perspective. It's about making us all right for who we are as unique individuals.

Why we feel wrong

We've been asked our whole lives to "understand others" and especially in their expectations. If we don't fully comprehend what they want from us, sometimes we don't even ask for clarifications. We simply reply: "Yes, I got it."

Maybe as a child your parents or teachers asked you to get your chores or homework finished or stop bothering a sibling or classmate. Their request could have sounded like this: "What are you doing? I told you not to do that. Do you understand me?" We might have followed their instructions but not necessarily "understood".

As we got older we were asked to "understand others" and epecially in their emotions.

How many times has someone sobblingly confided: "You don't understand me."

How many times have you desperately whined: "You just don't understand me!"

When we don't understand, we feel confused, frustrated and incapable. When we don't understand, we want to find someone else for solidarity who doesn't understand either. That way they can tell us: "Oh, he's so hard to understand, don't worry about it. No one understands him." Then we felt relieved and "right".

Worse than "not understanding" is the feeling of "not being understood"! Let's look at some statistics.

One of the top 3 reasons stated by 90% of suicide survivors as to why they attempted suicide was because they felt misunderstood emotionally and that they felt like the people close to them underestimated what was going on inside of them.

Food disorders are unexpectedly on the rise. Around 75% of American women confirm some unhealthy thoughts, feelings or behaviors related to food or their bodies. It is a fact that there are a lot of emotions tied into eating and physical appearance.

Almost 10% of the adult population in our society is depressed. It can be a chemical side effect of many things but look at what the word means. In latin it is "to take to a lower level". Literally, depressed people put "pressure" on themselves feeling weighed down by the expectations they put on themselves. It is just they don't have the skills or mindset to reach them.

All human beings have a deep yearning to be understood. In my opinion it could be even stronger than the yearning to be loved. With love, specialists state that humans are happier feeling love flow out of them. With understanding, they want it to come to them.

Guiding Principle

"It is impossible to be understood by another human being!
Stop wasting your life wanting to be understood by others.
Start living your life by understanding yourself."

Diana Dentinger

Take time and read that principle over again. How can this completely revolutionize your relationship with yourself and with others? It is not a theory. It is a fact! You cannot understand another human being. Many assessments, profiles, and questionaires have been assembled to help people understand themselves.

But now the question becomes: "How much is your wanting to be understood keeping you from living who you are?"

After 20 years as a Corporate Trainer and Personal Growth Coach, I've met very few adults who really understand themselves. Most of the hundreds and hundreds of professionals I have trained were not able to name their top ten strengths. Most of them were in their heads rationally thinking about what role they did well. They were waiting for others to tell them what they did well. What I taught them was how to connect to their inner drive to understand their talents. Then use these to perform effectively and efficiently in their roles. So the only thing to understand is how to feel that drive!

How can you feel

For as much as the areas of self help and psychology have helped some people understand themselves, they have actually "limited" others. Many of their processes take you on a path of examining your thoughts, feelings and actions. They recommend first that you align with positive thoughts so you feel happier. Then once you feel happier this will make you naturally act better. The end result is that you are able to get what you want. Some gurus even say that positive affirmations are enough. With these you can just wait around for the higher vibrational thoughts to attract to you what you want! This is disasterously incomplete!

Often a psychotherapeutic path simply supplies patients with a perfect scapegoat to their problems by blaming someone in their family or it leaves them with the impression of needing constant "fixing". When patients are expecting relief and happiness but not getting it, they are prescribed "happiness pills" that only dull their vitality.

Part of being alive means having inner cravings and desires. We crave food and reproduction just like animals. And as human beings we crave to move purposefully towards a goal. We cannot have this dulled or turned off! Desire is so essential since it stimulates us to move and act. We use reasoning with desire too. When we desire to be healthy we think of ways to stay fit. We exercise to move our physical bodies. When we desire a loving relationship, we think of how to meet another human being. Then we move our emotions and our body to hug, touch and make love.

Philosophically speaking, the only purpose of desire is to continue producing desire. It is not meant to create attachment to an outcome, object or person. Desire creates more desire. When you desire, you feel alive!

There are a few things about desire to still understand. Desire is actually an effect, not a cause. There is something that proceeds desire. It is deeper than desire. When you connect with this then you have your personal key to happiness.

> Needs are what create all your desires.
> Needs are what drive your behavior.

What are your Needs

Need is at the root of everything. Abraham Maslow was the forefather with his research on needs and motivation. He created the "Heirarchy of Needs" that explain the 5 needs common to all human beings.

"My research continues where Maslow left off.
My work focuses on your specific Individual Needs."
Diana Dentinger

Here is a brief description of the 22 Individual Needs that I have identified. Each Need has a specific Number and Name. There is even an example of a famous person who lived that Need fully so it is easier for you to make the association and see what it is like.

Read through the list now. Imagine yourself doing the verbs mentioned under each Need. Feel the difference between the descriptions. When you feel more inspired then check mark that Need as one of yours. Try to identify your Primary 3 Individual Needs.

Need Number 1 - Innovative

You feel the desire to start new things, to invent and to play.
Example: Marilyn Monroe: wasn't she playful and childlike?

Need Number 2 - Knowledgeable

You feel the desire to know, to collect information and to write.
Example: Mahatma Gandhi: wasn't he studious and well cultured?

Need Number 3 - Engaging

You feel the desire to converse, to charm and to create.
Example: Warren Buffet: isn't he one heck of a persuader?

Need Number 4 - Established

You feel the desire to lead, to possess and to delegate.
Example: J.K. Rowling: hasn't she become a leading novelist?

Need Number 5 - Conscientious

You feel the desire to guide others, to teach and to unite.
Example: Walt Disney: wasn't he always teaching a life lesson?

Need Number 6 - Selective

You feel the desire to illustrate graphically, to touch and to enjoy beauty.
Example: Leonardo Da Vinci: wasn't he all about beauty and fine art?

Need Number 7 - Adenturous

You feel the desire to demonstrate to others and train them to achieve.

Example: Sean Connery: isn't James Bond the epitomy of Multitalent?

Need Number 8 - Balanced

You feel the desire to honor others, respect laws and to decide.

Example: Mother Teresa: wasn't she incredibly dutiful?

Need Number 9 - Questioning

You feel the desire to analyze a situation, to diagnose and counsel others.

Example: John Lennon: wasn't he introspective and wise?

Need Number 10 - Dynamic

You feel the desire to move yourself, to catalyze change and progress.

Example: Bill Gates: do we need to mention all the advancements he stimulated?

Need Number 11 - Magnetic

You feel the desire to master things, to use courage and instinct.

Example: Thomas Edison: wasn't he all about power and energy?

Need Number 12 - Adaptable

You feel the desire to serve others and to offer a different perspective.

Example: Charles Darwin: didn't he talk about diversification in nature?

Need Number 13 - Radical

You feel the desire to transform, to revolutionize and restructure.

Example: Alfred Hitchcock: didn't he transform modern cinema with his thrillers?

Need Number 14 - Connected

You feel the desire to mediate, to befriend and to network.

Example: Mark Zuckerberg: isn't facebook about connecting?

Need Number 15 - Passionate

You feel the desire to investigate, to arouse creativity and to calculate.

Example: Martin Luther King, jr: wasn't he passionate about enslavement?

Need Number 16 - Expressive

You feel the desire to emerge, to celebrate and to burst out.

Example: Madonna: wouldn't you say she is about as expressive as it gets?

Need Number 17 - Entertaining

You feel the desire to shine, to give generously and take action in the world.

Example: Benjamin Franklin: didn't he leave an international legacy with his inventions?

Need Number 18 - Nurturing

You feel the desire to go deep, receive and perceive.

Example: Steven Speilberg: isn't he one of the most profound directors and screenwriters?

Need Number 19 - Supportive

You feel the desire to bulld, coordinate and support.

Example: Ted Turner: isn't he quite a successful philanthropist?

Need Number 20 - Inspired

You feel the desire to wonder, compose and renew.

Example: Federico Fellini: wasn't he revered for his distinct style in filmmaking?

Need Number 21 - Independent

You feel the desire to live your potential and set yourself free.

Example: Alfred Nobel: didn't he honor outstanding achievements?

Need Number 22 - Original

You feel the desire to live the moment, to depart and risk.

Example: Christopher Colombus: wasn't he the risk taker visionary?

You might have the same Need Number as another person but you will always express it differently for the combination of all your Needs together. You are a unique individual.

You cannot be put in a box or on a chart.
You cannot be described as a type or style.
You are multi-faceted.

Working with your Individual Needs is the only way to fully step into your power. Your thoughts, feelings and actions are predictable when you can identify your Needs.

No one else can feel your Needs.
No one else can imagine your desires like you imagine them.

Where your Needs come from

Your Needs stem from an "unhappy" story in your genealogy. At conception you receive this as an emotional memory. It's not a long drawn story in one of your ancestor's lives. It's actually only an 8th of a second. It's an "unhappy" instant.

What you receive is the image of this instant and it is placed in your subconscious. Your brain runs mostly on automatic pilots so it will rerun this instant! That's why it is so difficult for us to be in the present. We are run by our emotional memory. The problem is that often it has nothing to do with who we are in our wholeness, nor where we are in our particular context.

The 22 Individual Needs described above are the opposite of the memory you received. They are the "happy" endings. When you focus on the desires and feelings of fulfillment through living the Need then there is no need to analyze or point out anything else.

Awareness of your Individual Needs is vital.

Once you are fully aware of your Needs then you run your programs and your life. Instead of letting the subconscious run the show, you consciously chose what to do in this game of life! You finally have free will.

What to do with Needs

When we don't understand someone, often we give them a label. Let's say you have a child who "never shuts up". What if you parent or his teachers understood that this is because he has a Need to communicate. Wouldn't that change your perception of why he talks so much? Could you find ways to support your child in living this Need? Wouldn't that help you point your child in the direction of his life?

I have many clients who were talkative kids and are now great sales reps and PR people. These professions require a lot of communication skills. And these skills come natural to a person with a Need to talk!

Your innate Needs are your innate Talents.

IIn my Corporate Training business I work with Teams. Through the explanation of Needs, each team member sees first his individual strengths and then together they create a common language. In one company last year they were able to save 1million euro in waste products simply because they knew how to leverage each other's strenghts, communicate better and stay engaged with the company objectives. We formulated a mission statement based on the combination of the predominant Needs of each member. What a win!

Needs cannot be judged. They just are. So what do you get to do?
Satisfy your Needs.
Communicate your Needs.
Live the full potential of your Needs.

To make working with Needs fun think about the comments others make about you. The next time someone says something like: "Why aren't you ever home?" then you can kindly answer: "I need to move. I have the Number Need 10. You can't understand and that's just fine. Want to come with me?"

Remember these 3 vital things

1. You can never fully be understood by anyone else. You can only understand youself. Fulfilling your needs brings fullness even to your relationships and your profession.
2. You are your most valuable resourse. You have untapped resources that you are not aware of until you discover the depth of your Needs.
3. Only you can nuture and cultivate your Needs. Others are not responsible to satisfy your Needs. The more you apply yourself in your Needs the more you contribute to the world.

Take action on your Needs

1. Reread your Primary 3 Needs. Make a list of desires based on the Need Number descriptions. What do you feel like doing that would make you feel more alive right now?
2. Ask the people around you what they think your top 3 Number Needs are. Ask them if this helps them understand you better and understand what makes you feel happiest.
3. **Take the Innate Needs Quiz to enter my contest!**

On August 21st I will pick 3 winners to receive individual coaching from me. The value of this coaching is over $15,000. The work I do with Needs is fun, profound, symbolic and transformational. Everyone will be notified by email about the contest results. Best of Luck!

Special Gift

Discover your specific individual needs now!
Take the Innate Needs Quiz at:
www.dianadentinger.com/quiz

DAN FOWLER

BIO:

Dan has been a creative video and writing professional for the past 20 years and truly understands how to craft the Perfect Story, not only for business, but for one's life as well. He started his production company from the ground up, and truly believes in his company's tag line, "Believing is Seeing".

Dan is a black belt in Kempo and has a love for playing the drums, harmonica and singing his heart out. Dan has performed on the stage and in film and is the writer of 28 feature length screenplays, four of which being optioned by Hollywood studios.

Dan's fundamental goal is to bring laser focused attention to all who seek to be unstuck from their past and would love nothing more than to rewrite their story through his proven 7 Pillars of the Perfect Story System. He helps his clients embody their inner story and be unshackled from the limiting beliefs of their past.

GENIUS PROFILE:

Name: Dan Fowler
Biggest Challenge/Obstacle Overcome:

A frantic call for help on LinkedIn from one of my contact regarding his best friend's son. The son is terminally ill with cancer and his birthday was coming up and he and his family love the band, Maroon 5. The LinkedIn contact was pleading with anyone who could help connect this boy with his favorite band, Maroon 5 in some way. Most responses were generic, suggesting to go through their publicist, etc. I quickly responded to the post and told him there was a chance that I could get the boy direct access to Maroon 5 because I know someone who is best friends with the lead guitarist. Long shot, but over the course of 2 weeks, I was able to set up a special video message to this boy from Maroon 5 from backstage of one of their shows in LA. I was able to be a part of giving a sick boy and his family a dream come true.

Top 3 Favorite Foods:
Homemade Vegetable Lasagna
Tuna Casserole
Vegan Sweet & Sour Chicken

Top 3 Favorite Musicians/Bands:
Seether
Nickelback
Maroon 5

Top 3 Favorite Places Visited:
Budapest, Hungary
Prague, Czech Republic
New York City, New York

Bucket List Item Not Yet Accomplished:
Director a feature film that I wrote
Travel to Russia
Travel to Istanbul
Enjoy a Mediterranean Cruise

Top 3 Role Models or Heroes:
(tough one... have always marched to my own drum. I have never sought to emulate a Role Model or Hero. I always viewed myself as my own Role Model and Hero)
But... People that have stuck with he through thick and thin:
Amy Pattin, the love of my life
Kell Horton, unconditional friend
Sheevaun Moran, unwavering mentor

3 KEYS TO UNLOCK THE STORY BEHIND YOUR BUSINESS

by **Dan Fowler**

Story is in my blood. It courses through my veins with unbridled enthusiasm, but I know that I am of rare breed. Most people do not have the natural skills to convey a compelling story, but those that do seem to have more friends, get the promotions at work, and live a more fulfilled life compared to their non-story telling counterparts. Why is this so? The answer to this question is subtle, but very clear. People that can convey a story which not only resonates with their audience, but draws them in on an emotional level, are seven times more likely to create a "favorable outcome" from the story they tell.

A favorable outcome can be laughs at a well executed joke, standing ovations for an inspirational speech, or sales conversions from a well crafted social media post or email correspondence. Life in general is about creating as many favorable outcomes as you can and as consistently as you can, regardless if we are dealing with life, relationships or business acumen.

Unfortunately, the business arena has been sorely neglected when it comes to training and implementation of a powerful business story that can generate those favorable outcomes that we are all looking for in our companies.

You need to view your business as a living, breathing entity. It has wants, desires, goals, and most importantly it has a story. Not just the story you plan to write about your business' accolades and achievements in the future, but the back story that birthed this business of which you now find yourself a watchful parent.

Your business story is the heart and soul of your business' success. To put it another way, without a perfect business story that compels prospects to engage your core competencies, all you have is pretty business cards, a slick website, and an empty facade that is held up by nothing more that strategies and tactics. Don't despair, strategies and tactics are very important, but they make up only 1% of your business infrastructure. The remaining 99%, the part that most business owners neglect, is all about the internal story that drives the company's vision, innovation, and acquisition of new clients.

Story is everything. It aligns who you are with where you came from, and clears a path for where you and your business want to go. Story not only brings clarity to you, but also to your prospect that you work so hard to attract. Without story, your strategies and tactics have nothing to fuel their systems. Without story, you run the risk of being misunderstood in your marketplace, and without story, your business will not resonate with the clients you are called to serve.

To help you bridge the gap and truly ground yourself in your business culture, I am going to share with you 3 keys that will unlock the story behind your business in an authentic and efficacious way.

Story Key #1: Your Business Is About The **WHY**, Not The **WHAT**

I can't count the times that I have said to a business owner, "Tell me about you business." and they blather into a laundry list of all the products and services that their company offers, complete with prices and options, and they even spell out their website address. They think that they are doing a great job of "networking" and that they are telling me exactly what I want to hear because I said, "Tell me about your business". But they grossly miss the mark.

Your unique selling proposition for your business is not about what products and services your offer. It is definitely important to know what is in your catalog, but the mere product you offer is not what drives someone to care about your business, let alone buy from you. This is where most businesses fall short. They promote the WHAT of their business instead of their WHY.

The WHY question is more compelling. It connects me to your company's heart, allows me to relate to you, and opens up a trust dialog about the WHAT that includes your suite of products. Without the WHY, I don't care about your WHAT. The WHY is your company's unique story connection between your prospects and your company's core values and your transformative approaches; plus it creates an organic bridge between what the prospect is looking for emotionally, to WHAT you are offering experientially through your products and services.

Prospects make buying decisions for two reasons:
Price Warriors: They want it now and for the best deal.
Thoughtful Loyalists: They naturally make the connection between the value of your company's WHY to the value of your company's WHAT.

Number two is how you create ferociously loyal customers who come back to you over and over because of the story experience you give them. You compel them to move into action. WHAT you sell is always secondary. You need to hook your prospects in the WHY conversation first, and they will consistently come to you for your WHAT.

One of my clients, David Heard, embarked upon starting a business called Love Flags. His company endeavors to create memorial flags for family members of past loved ones, both military and civilian. I met David at a big marketing event in San Diego, CA, and when I asked him to tell me about his business, I got the traditional response that was focused on WHAT he offered and not WHY he offered it.

I sat down with David, and within 15 minutes, I was able to shift his story from the WHAT of his business, to WHY he started Love Flags in first place. I quickly showed him that his WHY story brings the most credibility and resonance to him and his business and that his clients are not buying memorial flags for past loved ones, rather they are investing in a family legacy and heritage piece that transcends life and death. I helped him shift his story from the inanimate product to the immutable bond of family. We changed the focus from an after death conversation, to a celebration of family life conversation. This one small WHY shift radically changed how David was able to communicate about his business. Instead of selling products, the WHAT, he now sells the WHY, a connective experience through his products. His WHY now fuels his business instead of his WHAT, and the quality of client connections that he is able to make is now light years ahead of where he once was.

The WHY for your business is an essential component to your entire marketing and messaging campaigns that generate not only purchases, but client loyalty. Forget pretty online shopping carts, catalogs of products, or flowery descriptions of your programs and services. The best companies and the most acute company leaders use story to answer three simple, but crucial questions:

1. Who Am I?
2. Who Are We?
3. Where Are We Going?

Answer these questions for yourself and your business, and you will unlock the key of the WHY factor that your clients are attracted to.

Story Key #2: Converting Prospects To Clients Is An **INSIDE JOB**

Converting Prospects is not rocket science, but relationship science. I say science because it can be a learned skill even if you are the most introverted person on the planet.

The word science comes from the Latin word "*scientia*" which literally means "awareness" or "being connected or acquainted with". Interesting how science is really about having connected awareness about something. I like the word aware because it demonstrated that in order to truly connect with something or someone, you must be connected from the inside out. You cannot truly connect with anything from an outside, cursory approach and thus, a bond can never be made unless awareness is in the equation.

This universal principle is also true in the world of business connections and converting those prospects to new clients. It is more than a superficial association with a prospect, but an intimate exchange of values which provide a shared transformational experience. A prospect's interest in your company or products begins by helping them envision a pleasing difference from their current situation and shows them how they can experience this bliss with you and your company.

Prospects want authenticity. An awesome product will only go so far. The nuts and bolts of brand loyalty and customer satisfaction come you being on top of your internal story game. You must be open and transparent with your prospects and convey to them what is possible for them when they collaborate with you. It does not matter what kind of business you have, but those that master the heart game in business, will master their client conversion as a result.

Around the globe, millions of dollars are spent each year on training programs for male mid and upper level managers so they can learn how to harness their "feminine side". These programs don't call it the feminine side, but that is exactly what it is. They help these men tap into their empathy, compassion, and how to express themselves to fellow work mates, as well as, business prospects. Why all the training? Simple. It works! Conversions have gone up, office dynamics have improved between managers and their employees, and the company's bottom line has seen a positive surge.

I mention this so you can see the correlation between the inner game of emotions, feelings, and heart connections with the interactions with new prospects that you would love to have as your clients. Sales is not about convincing anyone of anything, it is about treating your prospects like you would treat a loved one, open, honest, compassionate, and able to give them heartfelt advice that helps to transform them. You just so happen to be selling them your product or service in the process.

Here Are 3 Tips That Will Help You Master Relational Enrolling:

1. The best way to begin any relationship is to give first before asking for anything. There are many ways to do this and there are no set rules or guidelines, so figure out what works best with your style and the culture of your company.

2. One scoop of diagnosis is worth its weight in gold. Advise in a way that leads to solutions for the prospect and then customize those experiences to meet specific needs.

3. This is the most important one. You may have been told that building these kinds of relationships take a lot of time and patience. This cannot be further from the truth. Here is an easy way to think about it: The more transparent you are to your prospects, the more trust equity you build with them. The story of who you are, the who of your company, and where we are going is the key here. Talk about the mistakes that you have made, what you learned from them, and how you understand the fear and trepidation that your prospect is feeling. Trust is birthed from this transparency.

Story Key #3: **SALES** Are Born Out Of **STORY**

Stories resonate in sales and business because of how the human brain functions. Michael Gazzaniga, a cognitive neuroscientist, has researched the way our brains process stories; how the left hemisphere fills in gaps for the right hemisphere. Our brains *desire* narrative continuity, which draws us to stories. We naturally want to fill in gaps of information so we can process it.

Both right-brained and left-brained approaches need to be explored depending on whom you may be talking to. This kind of information comes up when you start the relational process with a prospect and the give-and-take cycle begins to build trust. The story you tell may need to cut through to diverse audiences, and the varied ways individual brains prefer to receive information. Bottom line is that all brains crave story whether slanted right or left, so incorporating your core WHY story about you and your company is crucial in the trust building phase because without trust, there are no conversions of sales nor loyal clients created.

Here Are 3 Elements Of A Powerfully Connected Sales Story That Will Transform Prospects Into Well Paying Clients:

1. *A Sales Story Narrative Has A Beginning, A Middle, And An End.* You must discuss back story and the background of where you were, where you are now, and where you and your company are moving in

the future. You must let your sales conversations include a framing of what is possible for your prospect, why you are the best suited to help them navigate through, and describe clear positive outcomes that are in alignment with your prospect's needs and desires.

2. *Authenticity X 3.* Sales story has to be genuine. If you are looking to enrapture your audience or you are dealing one to one, you must speak to your strengths. Highly analytical? Use that to your advantage, but make the mundane data come alive. Make your WHY rational, yet visionary.

3. *A Sales Story Must Be Grounded In Reality.* You can pull wonderful stories of trouble and triumph from your own client list. Stories that can demonstrate how your generated a positive outcome for your client will help illustrate to a prospect that you are the perfect person to guide them through their journey.

In sales, you must be part negotiator, part artist, and part master storyteller. Your business depends on you to be excellent at sales, no matter if you call yourself a "sales person" or not. Sales are transactions, not merely with money, but with story currency. The more powerful your stories are, the more high end sales you will be able to make. Weak stories, get weak results because the trust connection has not matured. Make the storytelling acumen a priority. It is a sales game changer and it lives up to the hype.

Putting Story Into Practice

So how do you flip on the story switch for your business? It may seem so out of your comfort zone that you are recoiling away, but you are still here reading because you know that I am right. Story is the element that unlocks the trust factor for your business between you and prospects. More trust equity with prospects, more conversion of sales, and that is what business is all about. Remember, it is relational science or relational awareness. Be aware of your prospects need and desire to be enrolled by your story. They want to connect with you and your company, so make it easy for their brains to do so.

3 Action Steps You Can Take RIGHT NOW:

1. Step into your prospect's shoes. Take the time to paint a vivid picture of "What Is Possible" when they work with you and your firm. This goes back to the outcomes discussion. Be clear about the outcomes you can deliver and start talking openly about them with your prospects. Refrain from talking about your products, instead emphasize the "What Is Possible" dialog.

2. Once you have stepped into their shoes, make sure you can effectively articulate "The Problem" that your prospects face and reference the "What Is Possible" dialog to display the fact that you not only understand their situation, you also have the vision to solve their problem and bring them into a new positive outcome. A part of "The Problem" conversation is sharing your personal "Transformation Story". Prospects need to know that you have gone through this before and are capable of assisting others. This is an important one, for it glues the "What is Possible" dialog with a resonation factor that only comes with a personal "Transformation Story". Be approachable. Be vulnerable, and most importantly, be authentic. Your prospects will thank you by signing up for your high end services.

3. The last element of your sales story has to include the "We Are In This Together" conclusion. Again, you will be focusing on outcomes here, but in a very vested way. You will convey to your prospects why you are the best possible choice to bring them to their "What Is Possible" and through story elements such as testimonials, past client transformations, and visionary brainstorming, you will be invited to co-write the prospect's positive outcome. When done correctly, your prospects will be signing on the dotted line and becoming your newest clients.

One of my first ever coaching clients was enrolled in this very matter. Regina was a hairdresser with an extreme artistic flare. She was wonderful with hair and makeup for both male and female clients, but her aspirations laid firmly in becoming a well known and respected film and television hair and makeup artist.

On numerous occasions, she tried to get her portfolio in front of the "right people" and even got a few interview requests, but was not landing the gigs in the industry that she so desperately wanted. Then she was introduced to me through a mutual colleague and after a short conversation, I quickly understood where she was and where she wanted to go. I then stepped into her shoes, and began giving her insights that she had never considered. She was a hair stylist, not a marketing negotiator, and I had strategies and techniques that would immediately bring her closer to the goal of working full time in the film industry.

She saw that I truly understood her plight and that I knew things that she did not. She needed my expertise to get over the hump that had been holding her back. I didn't sell her coaching packages, I sold her the future experience of achieving her goals through my proven system. This is key: I sold the experience, not the product or service. I sold the story that she so desperately wished to write for herself, but didn't know how.

Within three months, I was able to help her craft her inner story to match the outer story she wanted to manifest, and because of this understanding of her inner story, she could stand in the shoes of her industry interviewers and paint the picture of the hairdresser of whom they had always dreamed.

She embodied this new vision of herself and enrolled the people with whom she wanted to work into that vision. She is still a very successful hair and makeup artist in Hollywood because she mastered her story and brings others along for the experience.

To Unleash Your Business Potential, You Must Unlock Your Story

Special Gift

If you are looking for accountability with your business story so you can enroll clients into the experiences you offer, I would like to connect with you on an ongoing basis. I want to extend a complimentary subscription to my weekly affirmation program called, "Dan's Decrees".

"Dan's Decrees" is a 52 week program that gives you a weekly affirmation to focus on during the week, plus useful insights and techniques to guide you through the mastery of your own business story. "Dan's Decrees" will support you as you share your story with your prospects and enroll them into the experiences you provide.

All you need to do is go to my "Dan's Decrees" website:

http://www.DansDecrees.com

Fill out the easy form and plug in this exclusive code for readers of this book: **SELLWITHSTORY13.** This code will give your complimentary access to this program that is valued at $397.00.

I look forward to embarking upon this journey together and helping you craft your perfect business story to generate powerful profits through the experiences you offer.

DORINE KRAMER

BIO:

International Speaker and Author of the forthcoming book From Being Mom to Being Me, Dr. Dorine Kramer is passionate about helping stay at home moms whose kids have left the nest to reinvent themselves so they can make the next years the best years of their lives. Affectionately known as "Dr. Dorine" by her clients and colleagues, Dr. Dorine has created a unique process stemming from the lessons of her own life experience, where she moved from an exciting Medical Research career, to Stay at Home Mom, to International Speaker, Author, Business Owner, Coach, and Leader in the community. She believes that women who have been putting everyone else first deserve to know, love, and value themselves, so they can put their best foot forward in the world and lead amazing lives.

Now Dr. Dorine enjoys her grown kids, who think she is awesome and want to spend time with her, and she continues to build a deepening relationship with both her children and her husband.

Dr. Dorine received her medical degree from UCI and her further training in public health at UCLA. She now makes her home in Southern California, after having served as an epidemiologist at the World Health Organization, and the world renowned Centers for Disease Control (CDC) during the early stages of the AIDS epidemic.

GENIUS PROFILE:

Name: Dorine Kramer

Biggest Challenge/Obstacle Overcome: How come I don't get to list three of these? I'd say it's a toss-up between finishing medical school (and getting my license), and growing myself enough to soar from my empty nest.

Top 3 Favorite Foods:
artichoke
black cod (also known as sable fish)
home made super chocolate-y chocolate brownies with nuts (or maybe pistachio ice cream!)

Top 3 Favorite Musicians:

my father, who was a concert violinist; my mother, who was a singer (my parents actually met at a radio station where they were both performing;) then it gets tougher because I love so many in so many different genres of music--so here are a few: Leonard Bernstein; Itzak Perlman; the Beatles; Peter, Paul and Mary; Stephane Grapelli; Duke Ellington; Michael Jackson; and the list goes on, and on, and on.....

Top 3 Favorite Places Visited:
Dubrovnik
the Okefenokee swamp
almost any village in Scotland or Ireland.

Bucket List Item Not Yet Accomplished:

Improve my digital photography skills and use them on an African safari

Top 3 Role Models or Heroes:

I have no satisfactory answer for this question. There are certainly people I would like to meet and talk with, but I meet heroes every day and do my best to model traits of character and behavior that I admire.

REVEL-UTIONIZE YOUR LIFE!

by **Dorine Kramer**

Genius comes in many guises. You can be a genius at mothering, at gardening, at listening, at business, at knowing people, at anything that we as humans are capable of doing. Genius doesn't mean you are perfect, though, or that you do "it" perfectly. Merriam-Webster defines genius as, among other things, "a single strongly marked capacity or aptitude" and "a strong leaning or inclination." I wouldn't usually bother with a dictionary definition, but this one is important because it isn't how most of us would define the word. Did you notice it doesn't have anything to do with IQ? It's about something you *love* to do and that you do well.

When we look deeply into ourselves, and often when we listen to what others say about us, we all have genius, *are* genius. Did you know that about yourself? Well, now you do!

So knowing you are a genius, here is a big question for you. What do you stand for in the area of your genius? What do you believe? What are you committed to?

Have you ever really considered what you stand for? Or even thought about it at all?

If not, don't be surprised. And definitely don't start beating yourself up for it! It's so easy to get caught up in day-to-day living, in the busy-ness of caring for your family, earning a living, making dinner, cleaning house.... the seemingly endless tasks of modern life. Really contemplating the deepest reasons we do all those things may not seem necessary.

But *what's it all about, for you,* is a really good question, don't you think? Especially if you are facing an empty nest or some other time of transition, when the activities you've been doing on autopilot become less necessary or stop being necessary at all.

If you are a mom or dad with children still at home, I imagine you stand for your children—for loving them, teaching them, and caring for them in the best ways you know, and sometimes at whatever the cost. And I'm not talking about money here. Often the cost, particularly if you are a mom, is your Self: who you were before children came into your life, who you have grown into since becoming a parent, your self-esteem and self-confidence in who you have the capacity to be, who you want to be, what you want to do, and how to use your innate gifts, whatever they are, to leave the world a better place.

Well, I've walked in those shoes. The transition was tough but ultimately very rewarding, as it can be for you. And here's what I know now. I know I stand for women who have been putting everyone else first and have forgotten their own value. Until you can stand for yourself, I hold the space for you to REVEL in your life:

--Reclaim your Self;
--Expect and know you deserve to have not just what you need, but also
   what you want;
--Value who you truly are at your core;
--Explore and share your gifts, your own personal genius, with the world; and
--Love yourself fully.

Does any of this resonate for you? If so, you are one of my tribe. I welcome you with an open heart, open arms, and some tips and tools to help you on your way to the REVEL-ry you deserve in your own life.

Because this chapter is about *you* and *your* journey, and as I don't yet know you personally you might be wondering how I would know about your journey. Well, I've been there myself. As a physician I discovered early on that my primary interests were women, children, and public health (which is really a form of group medicine rather than the one-on-one medicine which you get when you go to see your doctor.) At the Centers for Disease Control, I was privileged to be part of the early task force investigating what we now know as AIDS. Later on I was honored to be a consultant for the World Health Organization. Still, I gave it all up when I had children, because being with them full time and raising them was what I wanted most.

But, and it's a big but, I lost sight of the fact that by exercising my genius at child-rearing, the children would grow up and want to pursue their own lives and dreams! And not only that, I also lost sight of me—the whole me—who had other areas of genius besides parenting to explore and share. I was so focused on my kids, teaching them, helping them, dreaming big dreams on their behalf, that when my full-time parenting role was downsized to occasional consultant, I had no idea who I was or who I could be, either personally or in relationship. I had no idea what I wanted to do and no confidence that I could actually do anything useful. Does any of this sound familiar?

My life became very small. I isolated myself from my friends, many of whom were reveling in their freedom; I told everyone, including my husband, that I was doing fine, which I wasn't (and we weren't!); I gained a lot of weight; and a lot of time passed almost without me even realizing it. Until the day when I realized I couldn't think properly. I couldn't participate in a complex conversation and I couldn't find words that I knew had been in my vocabulary before.

You know that old phrase "Use it or lose it?" Well I hadn't been using it (my mind, intelligence, etc.) and I was terrified that I had lost it for good. I panicked. And you know what? That was the best thing that ever happened to me. It was the catalyst for my journey back to myself and the joyful, rewarding and fulfilling life I lead now.

Now, I'm hoping this chapter is catching you before you find yourself on the sofa with a soap opera and a quart of ice cream for company. Whether it's an empty nest you are dealing with or some other major transition in your life, this chapter has some guideposts to help you keep your journey back to your Self on the quickest, easiest path.

In the following pages, you will meet your own unique internal guidance system, discover the very best way to enjoy an amazing life, and find out how to avoid some common pitfalls in your transformation. Use what I've learned and don't lose years of your life in struggle and denial before you find your own new or revived genius to make your life amazing.

USE YOUR GENIUS TO FIND YOUR GENIUS

Looking at the title of this section, you may be saying "Huh?" or "That sounds like gibberish!" So let me explain. There is more than one definition of genius. Here's one that's not commonly used, but should be: the spirit of a person that can influence her, kind of like a genie in a bottle. Only in this case, it's your own personal genie inside you. That sounds like something you can relate to, doesn't it?

Some other words for this spirit-genius might be intuition or gut-feeling. If you've done any personal development work you might have been asked to "go inside" yourself, or something similar, and that also is a way of connecting with that same spirit.

You come ready made with this spirit-genius within you. We all do. But here's the problem. You, like so many of us, have probably learned to override the internal, intuitive messages that come from your spirit-genius. For example, how often have you felt your mood lift at just the thought of being outside on a beautiful day? Did you go outside? Or did you deny yourself that pleasure because of the fifteen things on your to-do list that needed to come first? If you didn't go, I bet you felt grumpy or frustrated because you ignored the message, didn't you?

If you are like most people, you live an over-busy, often frenetic life in what feels like an unpredictable world. And in order to make your life run smoothly and feel safe and predictable, you mind makes choices using logic. You could probably say you've learned to live in your head, not your heart.

So what does that mean? It means when your spirit-genius shows up as an urge or a desire to do something that seems impractical or illogical, most likely you ignore it and do what seems logical instead. The trouble is, each time you do that, it becomes harder to hear the messages your spirit gives you.

So what do I mean when I say "Use your genius to find your genius?" Well, here's the thing. You have access to your very own personal spirit-genius, don't you? And it knows you better than you know yourself. It knows all about what the little kid inside you loves to do that you might have put aside because it's "illogical." It knows what you care about and what's important to you, even when you aren't consciously aware of those things. It always has your best interests at heart and it's always there for you, whenever you want to become conscious of it.

How about saying hello to your spirit-genius? Get in touch. Get re-acquainted. And be willing to explore some of those activities and ideas that are trying to get your attention. What does your spirit call you to do? I bet you have some thoughts that seem too frivolous or maybe even out of character, don't you? Consider that they are worth exploring. You might find out that your true Self, your genius in the world, lies in that very thing that has always made you say "Who, me? I could never do that." Really? What's stopping you? It's a great place to start.

MAKING YOUR REVEL-UTION AMAZING

OK. So let's say that now you're paying attention to your spirit-genius. You try something and it doesn't go as well as you planned. It's not amazing. Now what? Do you blame the universe for not being fair? Say it's all because of the economy? Blame your husband or your wife for not understanding you? Or maybe just give up?

Listen up, here, because you're about to find out a huge secret to making life amazing. It's a new way to think about the things that happen in your life and it will change everything for the better, if you let it.

If this book had music, there would absolutely be a fanfare right here!

So here it is—the big secret.

GIVE YOURSELF THE GIFT OF RESPONSIBILITY. Now that might sound a little obscure, so let me explain.

The best way to have an amazing life is to take responsibility for everything in it, while at the same time avoiding judgment and blame. When you take responsibility, that puts you at cause, and gives you the power to choose to do it differently next time. Would you rather hold the power, or be at the mercy of fate? I know what I choose.

Now, you might already be denying that it's even possible to be responsible for everything. I get that. That's where I started out, too.

But here's the deal. Being responsible puts you at *cause* for what happens in your life, rather than at the *effect* of someone else's actions. It means you can stand tall and say OK, that happened. What was my part in it, and what could I have done differently? Having the power means you are stronger than whatever the externals are in your life. And strange though it may sound to you now, it is the much more comfortable psychological place to be and will bring you both internal peace and external respect provided you don't blame or judge yourself or anyone else in the process.

Have you ever noticed that nasty little feeling lurking in your belly or your chest when you are late to meet someone? Or maybe you and your mate have been fighting about something and no one is willing to back down? That niggly feeling goes away when you simply acknowledge your part in the situation. About the meeting—you could have left earlier, right? And about the fight, the best solution is often to say "I'm sorry this happened" and ask "What could I have done differently here?"

It's not about blame, and it's not about forgiveness. It's about accepting that you can't change the past, and realizing that you can change the future. From my own experience and that of my clients, it feels much better on the inside, to let go of being powerless and instead, take responsibility.

Now don't get me wrong. It can be challenging the first few times. But it's so worth it. Feeling in charge of your own life by taking responsibility truly is exhilarating. And wouldn't that make your life feel amazing?

HOW TO DERAIL YOUR REVEL-ATION

I'm sure by now you are keen to cultivate your spirit-genius and to experience how it feels to be the one holding the reins on your life. If you take the actions you'll find at the end of this chapter, you will begin to notice the changes right away.

But guess what? I'm sure you know that like any path, yours may have some pitfalls to avoid along the way. And I imagine you'd like a quick heads-up on what to watch out for, wouldn't you?

Whether you are going *From Being Mom to Being Me* in my program, or from being laid off or retiring to finding a new career or project to be passionate about, or from being half of a couple to being single, there are three critical areas where women in transition tend to trip up without some guidance. So, very briefly, here they are:

First, beware of isolating yourself and trying to do it all on your own. It may be embarrassing to be 40, 50, 60 or more years old, and feel like you don't know who you are or what you are "supposed to" do with your life, particularly if you have raised a family. And no one wants to burden their loved ones with their fear or confusion. But, it takes persistence and time to do the internal work necessary to explore your Self and your genius. It helps to have a friend, a life coach, or a mentor who has been through it, to shorten the journey and to remind you to believe in yourself.

Take responsibility for choosing your path and who you travel with. Use the tools that are available to you, like my complimentary gift to you that you'll see at the end of the chapter. It's not cheating to have support! As President Obama said, **"No one can do it for you, but you can't do it alone."**

Second, this journey takes courage. Believe that you have what you need inside you. It's an incredibly exciting and rewarding journey, and you will need to leave your comfort zone to do it!

As your coach, I suggest changing your language pattern by just one single word. Which one? Check out how different it feels to say "I get to" instead of "I have to." Look at it as an adventure, or for fantasy fans like me, perhaps a noble quest. Yes, it might be unsettling to look into some corners of your Self that haven't seen the light of day for a while, but consider what you get as the end result. Wouldn't it be worth it to know exactly who you are, be in touch with your spirit-genius, and be clear on what you want in your life?

Third, you may find that some of your new priorities challenge who you have been and what you have been doing. If you've identified yourself as a stay-at-home mom, for instance, and your children aren't at home any more, your priorities have to change, don't they? Most often, your new priority should be to focus on yourself. Become the most interesting, exciting and excited person you can be.

Whatever transition you are making, it will be more successful when you re-examine your priorities with an eye to what you stand for now. Are you willing to take on the challenge? Embrace the shifts in values, expression and focus that are part of what you stand for now, and you will become who you need to be in order to take that stand.

On the next pages, you'll discover three action steps and a free gift to get you on track to REVEL in your Self and your new-found inner genius. I truly can't wait to hear how your life is transformed when you follow through on them!

YOUR THREE MOST IMPORTANT TAKE-AWAY POINTS

1. If you are in a time of transition–empty nest, retired or fired, newly single—it's your time to explore and pay attention to your internal spirit-genius to find your Self, your purpose, and what you stand for.
2. The biggest secret of an amazing life is to take responsibility for everything that happens. That puts you at cause and gives you the power to choose how your life will unfold.
3. Make sure you have a support system to get your Self and your genius out into the world in the quickest and easiest way possible.

QUICK AND EASY ACTION STEPS TO GET YOU STARTED

1. Every time you find yourself saying "I have to...." change it, out loud, to "I get to...." and notice how much more positive and exciting your plans are.
2. Start noticing who or what you blame when something in your life (or work) doesn't go as you had planned or hoped. Then, being really honest with yourself, consider what part you might have played and how to get a different outcome next time.
3. Take a few minutes, at least once a day, to close your eyes, check inside, and ask yourself what you need to feel good in that moment. Then do it if it's at all possible! It might be something as simple as getting a glass of water, stepping outside to feel the sun on your face, or making a quick call to tell someone you care about them.

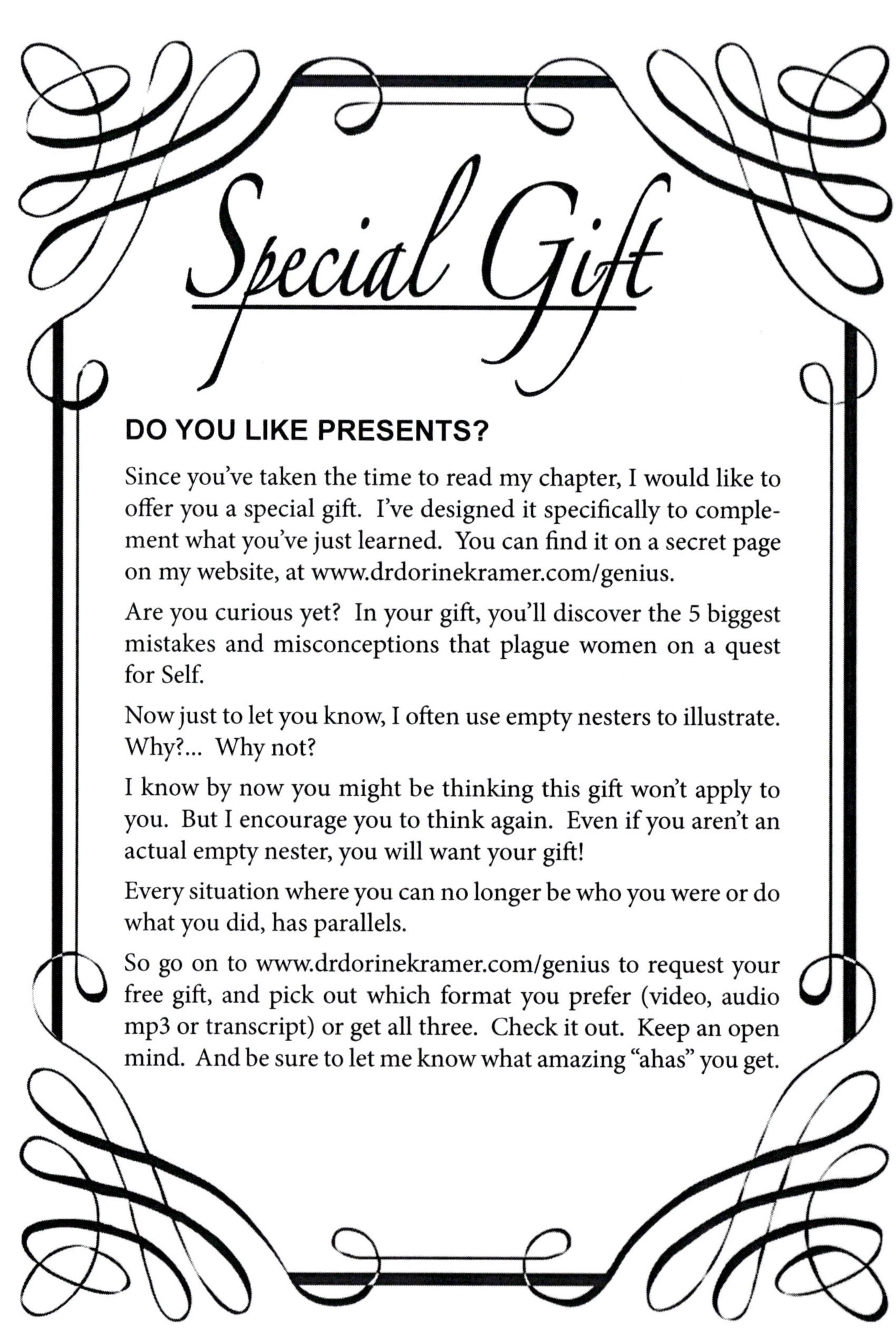

Special Gift

DO YOU LIKE PRESENTS?

Since you've taken the time to read my chapter, I would like to offer you a special gift. I've designed it specifically to complement what you've just learned. You can find it on a secret page on my website, at www.drdorinekramer.com/genius.

Are you curious yet? In your gift, you'll discover the 5 biggest mistakes and misconceptions that plague women on a quest for Self.

Now just to let you know, I often use empty nesters to illustrate. Why?... Why not?

I know by now you might be thinking this gift won't apply to you. But I encourage you to think again. Even if you aren't an actual empty nester, you will want your gift!

Every situation where you can no longer be who you were or do what you did, has parallels.

So go on to www.drdorinekramer.com/genius to request your free gift, and pick out which format you prefer (video, audio mp3 or transcript) or get all three. Check it out. Keep an open mind. And be sure to let me know what amazing "ahas" you get.

DAVIS LAWYER

Bio:

Davis Lawyer is a serial entrepreneur who has a deep belief transforming business is the most effective way to solve the massive challenges facing our world. He is currently the President of The Aquarius Group, a business focused entirely on building conscious businesses through consulting services and capital placement. Davis is a graduate of the University of Southern California where he studied political science and branding, while operating numerous businesses. He currently resides in beautiful Boulder, Colorado, a hotbed for conscious businesses and innovative startups.

Genius Profile:

Name: Davis Lawyer
Biggest Challenge/Obstacle Overcome:

Being arrested in Mendocino County and losing all of my operating capital while running a legitimate business in the medical marijuana industry.

Top 3 Favorite Foods:
Salted Sea Bass
Oven Roasted Vegetables
Vegetable Burritos

Top 3 Favorite Musicians:
Garth Brooks
U2
Drake

Top 3 Favorite Places Visited:
Moscow, Russia
Eze, France
Rome, Italy

Bucket List Item Not Yet Accomplished:

Build a luxury cruise ship that acts as the corporate office and housing for The Aquarius Group.

Top 3 Role Models or Heroes:
Robert F. Kennedy
Thomas Jefferson
Andrew Carnegie

CONSCIOUS BUSINESS: THE NEW PARADIGM

by Davis Lawyer

A shift is occurring in the world of business. In the wake of corporate corruption scandals (think: Enron) and the wholesale failure of the banking systems that control the global economy, average citizens in the industrialized world have become significantly more aware the impact that corporate powers have on their everyday lives.

A new era of transparency is dawning, facilitated by instant access to information through the Internet. No corporation or government is safe from the rapid mobilization of dissent amongst the public they serve.

Customers are now able to change corporate policies by gathering public attention and support behind a particular issue. There are numerous examples of Change.org petitions forcing major corporations to change policies. One such petition forced Bank of America to rescind a policy of charging $5 per month on debit accounts.

In 2009, a man who's guitar was broken in transit with United Airlines created a music video to protest their unhelpful and uncaring customer support. The video was watched 150,000 times in the first day, and within 4 days, United Airlines lost over 180 million dollars for shareholders when its stock price plummeted 10%. United has since made changes to their customer service policies, but millions of people around the world still think twice before booking with them because of this one incident going viral.

In addition to the power of their voice, customers are beginning to recognize their greatest power: the power they wield with their purchases. One way companies are finding a competitive advantage is through tying their brand to causes and values their customers are passionate about. Having a product that solves a customer's problem at a competitive price is now a given in business; what is not a given, is what the company stands for and what values its major shareholders have.

As an example, TOM's Shoes has catapulted to success since it was founded in 2006 with a "one-for-one" model of giving a pair of shoes to poor children for every pair bought at retail. Shoe giant Sketchers recently created its own "one-for-one" brand called "Bob's Shoes," after recognizing the huge opportunity in attaching customer purchases to philanthropy.

As another example, the 1% for the planet movement has over 1000 corporate partners that give 1% of their net sales receipts to approved environmental non-profits around the globe. These retailers prominently feature their participation in stores and in their marketing materials because customers like knowing that supporting these businesses equates to supporting the environment.

Though far from being a market standard, the link between consumer purchasing behavior and the values and causes of companies they buy from is a rapidly growing phenomenon that cannot be ignored.

These new purpose-driven and values-based companies are becoming known as *conscious businesses.*

With these trends in mind, we set out to build a business, The Aquarius Group, exclusively for serving conscious businesses. All conscious businesses share three main characteristics:

1. Conscious businesses are driven by a **clear purpose that improves lives**, not by the pursuit of pure profit. Though profit is necessary for a business to thrive, conscious businesses recognize that the purpose of business is to improve other people's lives. *For conscious businesses, profit is just the automatic consequence of serving others*, not an objective in and of itself.
2. Conscious businesses **consider all stakeholders** when they make decisions. While conventional businesses only consider the effect of their decisions on shareholders, conscious businesses consider

customers, employees, suppliers, communities, and the environment in every decision they make. If a decision is not a win for ALL stakeholders, they do not make it.

3. Conscious businesses **give back** to the communities that support them and to individuals that are less fortunate through philanthropy efforts that align with their business purpose.

Our definition of conscious business is heavily influenced by the ideas presented in Conscious Capitalism by Whole Foods CEO John Mackey, and Creating a World Without Poverty: Social Business and the Future of Capitalism by Nobel Prize winner Muhammad Yunis. These books are helping shift the mindset about the potential of business as a vehicle for social good.

We believe that conscious businesses are the single greatest force for good on the planet. But what does that mean for entrepreneurs and business leaders today? What does it take to build a conscious business?

Building A Conscious Business

The choice to start or transform into a conscious business is a choice to adopt a very specific type of identity, focused on improving the lives of those you serve. It's about getting crystal clear on the reason you exist (purpose), how you are fulfilling that purpose (mission), what your fundamental beliefs are (core values), and what the world will look like when you fulfill your purpose (vision).

Here is a framework for crafting the four core aspects of your conscious business identity.

Start with the Vision
You don't have to be out to radically change the world to be a conscious business. This is a common misperception. All that is required is a genuine commitment to improve other people's lives in a clearly defined way.

Your vision is a narrative or simple statement that explains the problems you see and the way you believe things should be. It's a statement of how you would like for something to be, but does not include anything about how you would make it that way.

As an example, the vision for The Aquarius Group reads:

"We envision a world where the measure of success is not how many dollars are in your bank account, but how many lives you impact for good.

We envision a time where businesses respect their environment and use only the resources necessary to give every human being a life of abundance.

We envision a world where every job is meaningful and purposeful, because every business is committed to a clear purpose of serving other people."

Your vision could be as simple as, "I envision a world where busses run on time, so that people can have more time doing things they choose to do."

Whatever you envision, just be specific and write it down!

Draw out your Purpose

Your business's purpose is its reason for being. The purpose is the most core aspect of the conscious business's identity. It should be a constant in your business, the North Star that guides each and every decision and action.

Your purpose follows from your vision, and is often a distillation of it. Sometimes, the vision is so clear and concise that it morphs into a purpose statement.

For our company, The Aquarius Group, our purpose is "to create a world where conscious business is the only type of business."

To craft your own purpose statement, you can ask questions like:

What do I seek to change through this business?

What am I passionate about?

How do I intend to make the world a better place?

What can I add to the market that will improve other people's lives?

How can I serve others in a unique way?

For simplicity, the statement can read "The purpose of (company name) is to (what you will change and improve)."

Choose your Mission

In this framework, a mission statement is a very specific goal or objective to be achieved in service of your purpose. Mission statements will change over time as your company grows and becomes able to make in impact well beyond what you could conceive of at the time you first write one.

What's important with your mission statement is that you are very precise with your objective. Choose a specific group you serve, a specific amount of service you will do, and a specific amount of time you will do it in.

Putting a precise intention out into the world not only gives you a way to measure your success, but also makes it clear to the higher power what you are calling into being.

If the purpose statement is something more general like "helping chemotherapy patients keep their strength during therapy" the mission could be something specific like "to improve the lives of 1000 cancer patients in the next two years by giving them back their appetite." Do you see how much easier the second one is to measure?

For The Aquarius Group, our mission is "to equip ten thousand conscious business leaders with the resources they need to reach ten million people by August 2018."

Define your Core Values

Core values define the culture of your business. They are the practices you believe should permeate everything your business does. They are ideals that you stand for and integrate into your business practices.

When everything in the business landscape is changing, core values keep a business operating congruently with the purpose, mission, and vision.

At the Aquarius Group, our core values are 1) Purpose, 2) Transparency, 3) Sustainability, and 4) Philanthropy.

For some companies, core values are statements rather than words. Whole Foods is a conscious business whose core values are more prominent than their purpose or mission. If this area is clearer for you than some of the others, look to models such as Whole Foods to understand how you can build a business around core values.

--

This framework, though very useful, is just a framework. We used this framework in our business, and in our clients' businesses as an internal starting point; but when it comes time to market your identity to the world, it's ok to be creative, so long as you stay true to your reason for being and the ways you embody that reason.

Can Any Business Become A Conscious Business?

The framework discussed above is a great foundation for building a conscious business, but what about existing businesses that want to transform? Can a company whose products have very little to do with individual or societal health become a conscious business? Could a company like Coca Cola or Anheuser Busch choose to become a conscious business?

Coca Cola produces sugary beverages that have been linked to obesity, diabetes, heart disease, and a whole host of health issues that are plaguing industrial societies. Anheuser-Busch produces intoxicating beverages linked to major societal issues like violent crime, DUI deaths, and broken homes.

Both of these companies' beverages are linked to individual and societal problems. However, their products are not the *cause* of these problems. The cause of these problems is that individuals choose to use these products irresponsibly.

Millions of people enjoy and desire both Coca-Cola and Anheuser-Busch products in moderation. The products they have created have authentic value, because individuals value and demand those products.

It may be counter intuitive, but these businesses could absolutely choose to become conscious businesses, without having to change the products that they sell.

It is a good thing that we as consumers have the option to enjoy the products these two companies make. It is the hallmark of our abundant, industrialized countries that we have such choices.

What is not a good thing, is that these companies have very strong incentives to influence consumers to use more of their products than is healthy for them or for society. It is one thing for informed consumers to choose to use a product, knowing it has downsides. It is another thing for companies to manipulate the public through advertising to consume more of their products, even to their detriment.

Coca Cola and Anheuser Busch both measure their success by their profitability. Everyone in the organization has incentive to try and sell more and more of their products, even if doing so does not benefit their customers or the communities they are sold in. Because profit is their only measure of success, they are not conscious businesses.

Both companies already have mission, vision, and core values statements. What is noticeably absent from both companies is a commitment to improving lives.

So what would a conscious version of Coca Cola or Anheuser Busch look like?

The major shift they would have to make is in taking "improving lives" seriously. This would call into question the use of massive advertising budgets to increase consumption year after year. When mounds of data show that the way customers are using their products is having major, negative effects on individuals and society, they would have to take responsibility and educate their customers, even if it curbs their profits.

The key with all conscious businesses is being 100% committed to ensuring your business does more good than harm. Conscious businesses are profitable, but they will never choose profit at the expense of the people or communities they serve.

Any company can choose a conscious identity if they will commit to improving lives for their customers and communities as much as they do for their shareholders.

The evolution of business from a focus on profit to a focus on people and planet is in its infancy, but it is a trend that cannot be reversed. For businesses brave enough to step into the new paradigm of conscious business, the future holds great rewards.

I personally invite you to step into the new paradigm, as you feel called. Supporting conscious businesses with your purchases is a great start; starting a conscious business is even better. It is time for each and every one of us to stand with companies that stand with us, and let the rest fall.

MAIN TAKEAWAYS

The world of business is shifting rapidly. Customers have increasing power over the brands they purchase. Conscious customers are driving the emergence of conscious businesses.

Building a conscious business is primarily a choice about identity. Clearly defining the purpose, mission, vision, and core values are the necessary steps to having a clear identity as a conscious business.

Conscious business are distinct from conventional businesses because they define their success by how much they are able to improve the lives of others, rather than by how large of a profit they make each year. Any business, even ones whose products or services are not particularly "conscious" can become a conscious business if they choose to prioritize people over profits.

ACTION STEPS

Clearly articulate your vision for changing something. This is a narrative.

Draw out your purpose into a simple statement. "The purpose of (company name) is to (what you will change and improve)." This will define success as your business grows.

Define a concrete mission. Who will you serve? How many will you serve? What exactly will you do for them? In what time frame will you do it?

Decide on core values that are congruent with your purpose and mission. What kind of ideals must you uphold to be true to your purpose? What do you want your company culture to be built around?

Share your message with those you wish to serve.

Special Gift

The Aquarius Group consults, connects, and funds conscious businesses whose values are deeply aligned with our four core values of purpose, transparency, sustainability, and philanthropy. We live to support other conscious entrepreneurs.

If you are a founder or leader in a conscious business or business exploring a new, conscious identity, we are grateful for the opportunity to offer you a one hour business analysis. In our time together, we will assess your current situation, define challenges, and offer you actionable solutions.

If you wish to take advantage of our conscious business expertise through our complimentary business analysis, you can contact Davis directly by phone, e-mail or through our website.

303.223.3797

Davis@TheAquariusGroup.com

www.TheAquariusGroup.com

GWEN LEPARD

BIO:

Gwen Lepard is Chief Joy Officer of Genius Squared, a Master Healer, a Speaker, an Authority on Joy, Master NLP Practitioner and Trainer, Master Hypnotherapist and Bestselling Collaborating Author of "The Gratitude Book Project, Celebrating 365 Days of Gratitude". She is also the Host of Joyful Living Radio and Joyful Living HEALTH Radio, igniting, empowering and healing the healer within each of us. With close to 30 years of healing experience, she's impacted thousands of people through touch, voice, words and music.

Currently, she holds the position of Chief Joy Officer at Genius Squared LLC, an international training company. The position encompasses being the person that focuses on the positive and finding how things can go right as well as providing coaching and healing for clients and staff.

In her 9 years as an on-air radio personality she was featured in over 1500 shows and spoke in front of groups of hundreds and even thousands during a fundraiser featuring Heart's acoustic group, the Love Mongers. She's directly worked one-on-one with a number of well known musicians backstage and in the studio.

Gwen co-founded a small record label that included an album she personally placed in over 400 stores and through her efforts that album made it to the Grammy ballot in four categories.

As an Authority on Joy and a Master Healer, she brings healing through joy, removing shame and guilt as well as creating awareness of the damages of verbal abuse. Through her work with private clients, speaking to groups, running workshops, hosting Joyful Living Radio and Joyful Living HEALTH Radio, both found through www.joyfullivingradio.com, Gwen Lepard brings more joy to the world. She is shining light on a new way to have more energy, better health, happier relationships and how to become more attractive to everything you desire.

GENIUS PROFILE:

Name: Gwen Lepard

Biggest Challenge/Obstacle Overcome: My biggest challenge has always been myself. Being in my own way has been a reoccurring theme throughout my life and yet I live a life that is full and rich in experiences. With my father's passing this year, I've finally found the "boot to the seat" that, it's not about me, it's about who I'm here to serve and it's past time to get out and do it! Stay tuned for more…

Top 3 Favorite Foods:
Fresh organic produce
fish that is cooked in such a way that it melts in your mouth
my own homemade raw chocolate served with raw pecans.

Top 3 Favorite Musicians:

Tough one… Love music and musicians. Favorite song now, Rise, is by an artist named Shawn McDonald, Faith Hill, who I met one week before her breakout hit "Wild One" is up there, and Latin Jazz Musician, Mark Antoine, a definite fav.

Top 3 Favorite Places Visited:
Lake Tahoe, the lake itself and surrounding mountains, not so much the city.
Costa Rica, the Pacific side and was recently in DC would like to go back and explore more.

Bucket List Item Not Yet Accomplished:

Creating a movement to ignite, empower and heal the healer in each and every one of us and walking the Great Wall of China to bring worldwide awareness of the damages of verbal abuse. Probably will tie them together.

Top 3 Role Models or Heroes:

I'm inspired by the greatest healer that ever walked our planet, Jesus, the profound work of Gregg Braden, who I intend to meet soon, and when it comes to a Superhero, I truly adore Robert Downey Junior as Ironman…

BE THE SUN... HEALING THROUGH JOY

by Gwen Lepard

"Your Genius is Joy." That's what Eiji Morishita said to me one afternoon as we sat across the table having finished a very fine meal at the exclusive members club where we'd met. It was the first time I'd ever hired a coach and I had no idea what I was in for.

The meal had been spectacular. I'd ordered from the *left* side of the menu. You know, the side with the descriptions instead of the price.

How may times have you ordered chicken or pasta when what you really wanted was the dish that, just from the description, had your mouth watering? Have you even given yourself the joy of ordering from the left side of a menu? This was one of the things I was to discover in my new shift by hiring a coach who loves food.

During our session over that succulent meal, he'd discovered how I'd fled my home in Montana after years of verbal abuse had become physical. How I'd lost my home, my credit rating, the man, that I'd thought was the man of my dreams… How I'd lost myself.

I'd started rebuilding my life and was taking a course in self-development when I met, Eiji. My effervescent self had resurfaced and I was dancing on breaks and being joyful.

"You bring so many people joy, you need to have some joy yourself," he said. "Order whatever you *truly* want." Since, I too love food and I wanted to be coach-able, I did!

Then Eiji asked, **"What is the difference between happiness and joy?"**

At the time I didn't have an answer and I knew that without it I wouldn't be the "Joy Authority" that he'd named me. That question became a defining question, a question of distinction that took me over a month to answer.

Joyful Revelation…

There wasn't an exact moment when enlightenment came. At least, not one I recall. At first I was struggling with finding the answer consciously through introspection. You've probably had moments like this when you ask yourself a question over and over, thinking that the answer lies in your conscious mind. It can be pretty frustrating, can't it?

I knew there was a difference between happiness and joy, I'd just never thought about defining the two and creating a "distinction". Since the introspection wasn't working, I thought I'd try something new. I'd been studying NLP (NeuroLinguistic Programming) and so I stuck the question in my unconscious mind and said, "You figure it out."

One day, seemingly "out of the blue", an answer arrived. It was really more of a collision than an answer. I'll get to that in a moment…

A friend had noticed that I was a healer in the habit of over-giving. Someone would be in pain and I'd jump right in to provide relief. After a few sessions, I'd be exhausted and if someone else needed help, even if I was completely drained, I would dig deep to give them what they needed at my own expense. He was wise in the ways of metaphor and shared this with me… "Be the Sun!"

Huh? "Be the Sun?!" What the heck did that mean and how was it suppose to help me in my over-giving. How can it help you? I'm willing to bet there is no way you plan on becoming a fiery ball of molten gases. Neither was I.

He continued with some questions that brought clarity… "Is the sun diminished in any way by shining its light of warmth and healing upon us? Does it care if it shines and we turn our back on it because we'd rather be sitting inside at our computers doing social media? Is it an abundant source of energy? Yes? Then… Be the Sun!"

With those questions and declaration, I realized that I'd been giving from myself rather than from the completely available source of energy that we all have to draw on. And, I'm not alone in this. It's common among healers to give from themselves instead of from an abundant source. What is this source? Some call it Spirit, others the Universe, many God. My friend, he used the metaphor of the Sun.

So getting back to the collision that became the distinction and my definition of Happiness versus Joy… Seemingly out of the blue the words, "Happiness is feeling the rays of the Sun. Joy is being the Sun. Be the Sun!" arrived in my consciousness. Metaphor colliding with the question I'd tossed into my unconscious mind… I was ready to share the message of Joy with the world!

Have you had an experience like that? One where all of a sudden everything makes sense? Maybe you picked up a book and it opened to exactly what you needed to hear. Maybe it was taking a walk and connecting with nature in a way that you hadn't before.

Maybe it's your first child or maybe it's the loss of a loved one.

What?! How can the loss of a loved one help make sense of things? It's a very good question and one I found myself facing very recently. For me, what made sense is the awareness of the passage of time and how I'd found so many excuses for not doing just what I'd proclaimed only 2 paragraphs above… sharing my message.

If you've found yourself constantly searching for your "why" to get out there in the world and do what it is that you feel you have to share with the world, I'll have something for you at the end of the chapter. No, wait… Okay, if you must, go look, do what you have to do. Just stick your finger here so you can come back, because I'll be sharing more with you about how to "Be the Sun"… Also how sharing that message has helped other healers tap into an inner and outer strength that is helping heal our world.

As I took on the metaphor of, "Be the Sun", I found I had more energy and healings happened much faster. Also, I would find myself in places where there were people that needed to hear, "Be the Sun". It was amazing to me how it resonated and they really saw how it would impact their energy level and what they had to offer to those they were serving. As a result of sharing with others, a training course in Joy was developed and a radio show, Joyful Living Radio, came into being as well.

"Be the Sun" became a mantra and the distinction between Happiness and Joy became a platform.

Now, Happiness is a wonderful thing! There are many teaching and writing books on how to be happy. This is also very much needed for the healing of our world. The challenge with happiness is that it relies on outside sources. By definition, "feeling the rays of the sun," it is a feeling, an emotion at the mercy of outside influences.

"The weather's nice, Yea, I'm happy! There's rain today, Boo, I'm sad." You can hear these words or ones similar in the playground, at the office or in your own home. Maybe you've even said them yourself! So Happiness is a feeling… Like feeling the rays of the Sun.

Joy on the other hand is a Being… Like Being the Sun! Joy comes from inside us. We're born with it. It bubbles up and out of us from the day we're born. We, each and every one of us, come into the world complete with the Beingness of Perfect Joy. Love, light and purity are essential parts of who we came here to be.

So what happens? Life! Among other things, we all have our stories. Your story is yours and it's valid. Yet, if you could change it… Would you? What would it be like to embrace a simple little thing like… say, Being the Sun? How would life be different if you allowed yourself the choice to choose a different outcome in the story you've been telling yourself all this time?

As a child, you are the Sun. The whole universe revolves you, your wants, needs and your desires. You are a bundle of Joy! So to reclaim something that is your birthright, how easy can it be? For those who get the metaphor of being the Sun, it can be immediate.

As adults, we tend to complicate things. There must be some long complicated process or it has no value. Have you ever felt or said, "There has to be an easier way?" Well, there is and it is as simple as making a decision. In this case, the decision to Be the Sun, to choose Joy as your default. To reclaim the Joy that you came in with as an infant.

I see that Joy in Ema, who is Eiji's first born daughter. You see I went from being his client to working with him. He gave me the title of Chief Joy Officer and every where we go, people either say, they love that or that they need a Chief Joy Officer themselves.

Now, what the heck does a Chief Joy Officer do? By definition: The person in an organization that focuses on the positive. A Chief Joy Officer is the person who looks for how things can go *right* in every situation. What this does is provide another perspective from what typically has been a focus on how things can go wrong or the "what next" mentality. Certainly, training in NLP, an awareness of how language is used in communication and intuition are helpful in this position. However, a large part of what I do is maintaining the positive energy by Being the Sun, and providing healing as needed.

It seems that the journey from a girl who'd been beaten down to the point of totally losing her identity, to the joyful woman who's able to help other's with her story, skills and talents, with just being herself... To become the Chief Joy Officer to a powerful international speaker, has been a journey of a lifetime... And in some respects it has! However, in reality it's only been a few short years, highly impactful years to be sure.

If you were able to shorten your journey from the pain you're experiencing, be it physical, mental, emotional or spiritual, to living a life full of energy and joy, would you?

I know that earlier I mentioned that all it takes is a decision. And that is true! However, if you're looking for something a little more concrete, say, 5 Action Steps you could take, would that seem more doable for you? If you said, "Yes!" then read on...

Joyous Action...

5 C.A.R.A.T. Action Steps to "Be the Sun" and Shine your Light on a life you've created with less pain, less guilt and less shame. The Life you create now will have more Energy, Vitality and JOY! Like a diamond these steps come as a carat. The actual weight, quality and clarity is up to you.

1. Choose Joy as your default
2. Allow yourself to feel emotions as they come up
3. Release those emotions by naming them
4. Accept and embrace emotions that energize and support you
5. Take responsibility for the life you're living now so you can change your future

Choosing Joy as your default allows you to decide to respond in a positive light to the challenges life throws your way.

Allowing yourself to feel emotions as they come up clears the air and keeps them from being stuffed into the cells of your body, often in the back, neck and stomach, where they cause pain. They just want to be heard. When stuffed for too long, these emotions can even become disease.

Releasing these emotions is a simple as naming them. One of the formulas I use is, "I feel _______," with my clients creating, immediate pain relief and often, what seem like miraculous results.

Accepting and embracing the emotions that support and energize you, does just that! You have way more energy, your body feels lighter and you feel supported and heard.

Taking Responsibility for the life you're living now is key to being able to create the life you choose to live. To blame others for what you're now experiencing takes you out of the role of creator and we all have created the life we are currently living. Since you have the power to choose what you'd like the rest of your life to look like, "Choose Wisely..."

Joyful Conclusion…

In wrapping up this chapter I'd like to share 3 Key Takeaways. You may find more of your own and I encourage you to go back and reread as often as you like. Also, this little book is full of Pure Genius solutions and resources that I recommend you check out and see if they're a fit for you. I'm thrilled with the caliber of my fellow Genius authors and their big visions to make this world a better place.

Getting back to those 3 Key Takeaways…

First, what you just read: The 5 C.A.R.A.T. Action Steps to becoming a more joyful individual who has the ability to create the life you choose.

Second: Embracing the metaphor of "Be the Sun" can provide you with a source of energy to power the life you choose to create.

Third: Happiness is a feeling and Joy is a being. Be Joy… Be the Sun.

When asked, "How did you find out you're a Genius at Joy?" I say, I was told over an amazing meal. Remember, there I was sitting across the table from Eiji, at that exclusive members club, just finding myself again, having no idea what I was in for with this coach I'd just hired. After consuming what was truly one of the most delectable pieces of fish I'd ever eaten, paired with a salad that was the perfect foil, what I found was kindness, an intuitive sense of what would work for me and an awareness of Spirit that helped this healer become a Master Healer through Joy.

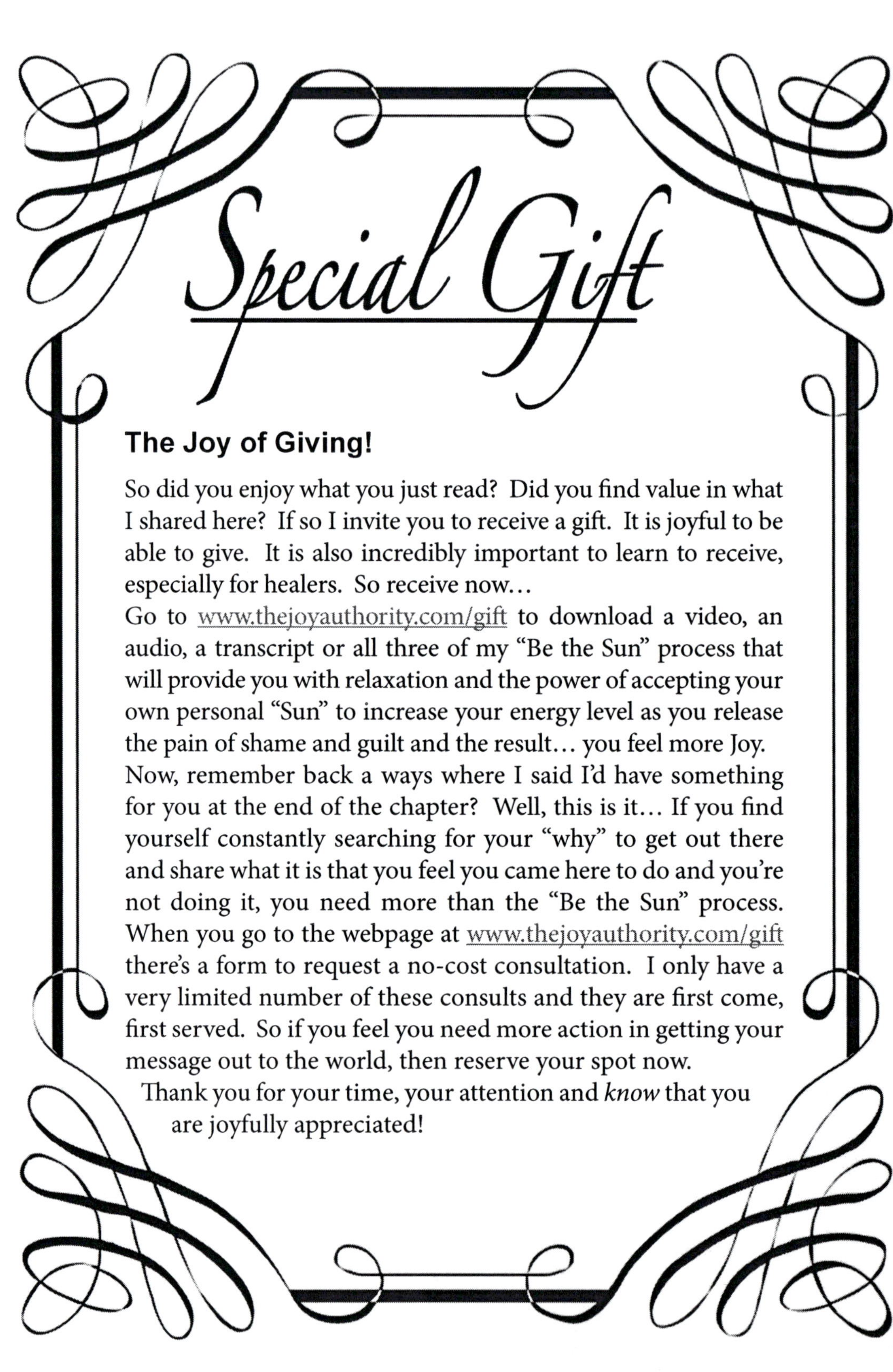

Special Gift

The Joy of Giving!

So did you enjoy what you just read? Did you find value in what I shared here? If so I invite you to receive a gift. It is joyful to be able to give. It is also incredibly important to learn to receive, especially for healers. So receive now…

Go to www.thejoyauthority.com/gift to download a video, an audio, a transcript or all three of my "Be the Sun" process that will provide you with relaxation and the power of accepting your own personal "Sun" to increase your energy level as you release the pain of shame and guilt and the result… you feel more Joy.

Now, remember back a ways where I said I'd have something for you at the end of the chapter? Well, this is it… If you find yourself constantly searching for your "why" to get out there and share what it is that you feel you came here to do and you're not doing it, you need more than the "Be the Sun" process. When you go to the webpage at www.thejoyauthority.com/gift there's a form to request a no-cost consultation. I only have a very limited number of these consults and they are first come, first served. So if you feel you need more action in getting your message out to the world, then reserve your spot now.

Thank you for your time, your attention and *know* that you are joyfully appreciated!

LANE LOWRY

BIO:

Lane Lowry is a skilled facilitator of raising consciousness and healing at all levels of one's physical, mental, emotional and spiritual being. He teaches a complete system of contemplation combined with a unique style of meditation and muscle testing which rapidly increases one's level of consciousness. His work is an evolution of his studies of several spiritual masters and expands on the teachings and accomplishments of Dr. David Hawkins.

Through Lane's simple yet detailed technique anyone committed to the practice can experience and maintain a higher level of consciousness. Most people who attend an event live or by phone describe feeling an uplifting experience of enlightened consciousness. Lane currently maintains an active client practice worldwide and leads meditations, masterminds, online seminars and various workshops.

GENIUS PROFILE:

Name: Lane Lowry
Biggest Challenge/Obstacle Overcome:

Escaped the ordinary into Enlightened Consciousness

Top 3 Favorite Foods:
Raw Food
Vegan Food
Custom Power Foods

Top 3 Favorite Musicians:
Wah!
Jason Mraz
Luminaries

Top 3 Favorite Places Visited:
Hawaii
Alaska
Lake Tahoe

Bucket List Item Not Yet Accomplished:
Tour Vatican City, Write the definitive guide on attaining Enlightenment, Create a Resort Community with a healing and healthy lifestyle component.

Top 3 Role Models or Heroes:
Jesus
Buddha
Krishna

HIGH CONSCIOUS AWARENESS

by **Lane Lowry**

High Conscious Awareness is a state of being that is characterized by peace of mind; feelings of joy; incredible insights; courage to be a leader; a passion pursue goals and dreams. This powerful awareness is the description given by many people after hearing just a short presentation and a brief meditation. The fundamental principles for obtaining this enlightened state of consciousness are summarized here.

The subject of high conscious awareness is focused on Enlightenment in both a traditional and spiritual sense of the meaning. Traditionally it means to obtain a high state of special knowledge. Thinking and perception becomes very clear with the ability to discern incredible insights from events and energies. The spiritual experience is one of complete connection to all that is and awareness of the soul and its role with the body.

An enlightened person transcends the traditional view of "me" separate from "others" and begins to see the value and quality of all beings and things. This facilitates the release of judgments, fears and egocentric frustrations. The person tends to exhibit a humility and self confidence that defies any "reasonable" person's examination. A person who has attained this state is in a class of awareness commonly called Enlightenment also known as Buddhahood, Self-Realization, Satori, and Moksha.

Does this interest you? Nearly everyone says "Yes!" But our discovery is that you must "intend enlightenment" which is a much different matter than desire. Most people experience desire as "wanting" which they experience lack and the inability to obtain it.

If you were to "set the intention for enlightened consciousness to flow through" you tell the mind and consciousness that you are willing to allow that energy to flow through you. This is very powerful because consciousness is energy, like a powerful wavelength of communication, attracted and delivered to you when you are "dialed in" like a radio, to that frequency. This signal becomes infinitely larger for all practical purposes as consciousness goes up and you become conditioned to handle that higher energy.

To increase consciousness you must also purify the consciousness. Those who have practiced some form of fasting or cleansing know the value of "purification" and its potential to create well-being and health. Here is a simple way to view it for consciousness. When the awareness is pure, free of negativity, there is a flow of joy, happy feelings, high energies and calm thoughts. It also holds true for the body. When the consciousness is pure the body tends to experience well-being free of pain or discomfort. Typically there is a state of high energy and when resting a deep rejuvenating sleep.

To completely purify consciousness you must become unencumbered by other "energies" that would intercept or deflect the enlightened consciousness. This is extremely important to understand in light of the terms "positivity" and "negativity." We wish to release any and every aspect of consciousness that is not our own to experience the flow of high conscious awareness. This means any negativity AND any positivity, simply to be yourself, one hundred percent yourself and nothing more or less. You, as a perfect "antennae," for higher consciousness.

This point of releasing everything that isn't you is important. Many people seek to "collect" or "connect" with other well meaning energies of great masters, saints, religious leaders, guides, angels, teachers, entities, etc. This proven system delivers only one thing, your personal enlightenment, completely free of any other being, energy, teaching or commitment, it is simple and pure. Please give it a try and set aside for now all you have been taught about how to obtain happiness and high consciousness.

Here is the intention that must be set to obtain enlightened consciousness:
   "Please set the intention for enlightened consciousness to flow through,
   to experience the purity of my own consciousness and
   to cast out any expression of consciousness not fully my own."

Say this upon arising in the morning and throughout the day. Saying this often is very important because a person nearly always has the opposite of the intention for enlightened consciousness, even moments or just seconds after "setting the intention." What causes this loss is what lowers our consciousness, subjects us to mental harassment of our own monkey mind and leaves us emotionally spent, upset or dis-empowered.

Quite literally, it was the pursuit of feeling good all the time and the discovery of what takes out the intention for enlightenment that created this simple system. What was created was a set of tools that are accurate and specific to release blocks in the physical, mental, emotional and spiritual realms.

The system will not allow any deceptions or misleading answers. This is really a key point because most people are aware that they don't really know the whole truth. When people attempt to validate something as truth they usually use reasoning, the generally accepted viewpoints of others, or how they feel. This system, in contrast, relies on your personal truth and you will know exactly where that is and how to find it.

In order to discuss the concept of personal truth, there are two critical elements to be clear about. First, a person must learn what is "constructive" for them and second, what is "destructive" for them. Constructive is life affirming and positive for them while destructive is life degrading and negative for them. An example of this is easily seen in environment as one person's food is another person's poison. When it comes to consciousness itself, you must know what is constructive or destructive to our soul to bring your soul and consciousness into enlightenment.

When it comes to determining your personal truth, there is simply the act of discerning what is constructive over destructive. This must be done with muscle testing also called muscle checking which bypasses the personal will or ego and accesses the information at higher levels of consciousness. This information exists before the personal will and ego and is considered the personal truth. Constructive or positive would be true and destructive or negative is not true. Do not equate not true with false.

Muscle testing is used for many health care techniques such as Applied

Kinesiology and Chiropractic. It has been proven effective for many health-care practitioners and shows success in multiple studies. It is simple to explain and perform. A person extends an arm and resists while another person applies a small amount of pressure after making a statement. If the statement is "true" for the tested person, their arm will remain strong (positive), if it is not true then the arm will be noticeably weak (negative).

This simple testing method can vary in its accuracy and consistency. Through years of research by the author a shocking discovery was made that specific types of negativity block accurate muscle testing AND the attainment of enlightened consciousness. Cataloging and carefully creating corrections for these resulted in a very effective system for accurate testing. This has been perfected over years of clinical use as scores of people attained enlightened consciousness.

As a person develops this skill, consciousness will increase and the powers of contemplation grow with the ability to discern nearly anything in reality. Even more exciting is that a person can learn to perform this test themselves without a partner and can apply the tests for any aspect of their physical, emotional, mental or spiritual Self. For detailed training please contact the author.

Even a beginner can be effective with the technique for basic tests and it is now time to get started. Simply make the statement "Intends Enlightenment" and test the arm. If it is strong, we say "positive," you are on the right path. If it is weak, we say "negative," you are in need of setting the intention.

Just by reading or saying the intention people report that they can feel layers of energy lifting off of them. Please try it yourself. My recommendation is to say it at least 20 times per day at first, more is better. When you have found that you can maintain the intention for enlightenment, by showing "positive" for the statement "intends enlightenment," then you will usually notice that you feel and perceive the world in a positive manner and superior to the time in which the statement tests negative.

Once you have control of this simple and extremely important aspect of your will and consciousness, your sovereignty over your body and consciousness will grow. What most people soon discover is that they can literally will away conditions that cause them disharmony in their body and life. They also discover that they have a massive ability to harness the law of attraction for the manifestation of their desires.

The ability to heal tends to grow as love for oneself and the world overcomes the negativity. This applies to physical pains, age old health concerns, negative emotions and mental conditions, especially the release of anxieties, worries, concerns and judgments of Self and others.

While the topic of health and healing is at the top of most any persons list of concerns, it is usually the most disempowering conversation because the body seems to just do its own thing. We all know or perceive a mind and body connection but how do we fully harness this and become the "cause" that creates vibrant health and well being? The answer is that our consciousness is the controller of much of our physical body. The "instruction" manual that is your DNA is "information" and as your consciousness goes up, your instruction manual becomes more clear and concise due to more "constructive" energies.

There are many valuable insights about higher consciousness which apply to the realms of thought and emotions, too. What we find with increasing levels of consciousness is that the majority of the thoughts which create discomfort and negative emotional response simply are not present. While it is clear that they existed in us before enlightenment, somehow they are not present after the rise in consciousness.

The state of fewer thoughts in the mind is similar to what spiritual aspirants report as their results after long periods of meditation. What is most commonly observed is that there is a trust in the universe to provide, that creates a deep peace and goodwill for ourselves and others. The fundamental component of the Ego, for survival, is somehow completely rendered cooperative and non-judgmental.

Once the state of enlightenment begins to settle into the day to day thoughts and lifestyle, each and every aspect of daily life becomes infused with the beauty and sanctity of the creation and creator. While there are many movements and religions that have excellent descriptions and prescriptions for attaining this experience in this lifetime and beyond, the actual experience validates and updates the meanings and depth of these timeless traditions.

For me personally, my depth of appreciation and deep love for the spiritual masters, particularly mine of my birth and upbringing, shone through and all doubts were wiped clean. It is beyond faith and more like a deep knowing with complete joy and assurance. That experience alone leads me to beg people, literally, to pursue enlightenment, so they can experience the amazing touch of the divine.

To talk about Enlightenment or some state of higher consciousness without talking about religions or saviors would be incomplete. What you can be assured of is this. You can check the validity and accuracy of the creation and its creator with your own "personal truth." While doing this very task many people blossom into states of impermeable love and faith.

The experience of seeing people strip away their doubts and fears about their shortcomings, their path, their future and how this all affects those that they love is profound. The restoration of their faith and the path of religious pursuit, if it interests them is amazing. Please allow yourself the opportunity to experience this, you will thank yourself for the gift.

The act of contemplation is a fundamental activity of this system. The thought processes that bring higher awareness include many "spiritual subjects" especially related to the soul and what to check in your awareness to release. You must have a solid system for accessing your personal truth and clearing off negativity from your body and consciousness. This means you must be properly trained in muscle testing. Don't waste your time looking elsewhere, take the time to get on a call or attend a meeting with me, you will know in one session if this is for you.

Let's dive into the subject of meditation. For most who have tried it and few who have a regular practice, you know the power of it and the frustration that can come with it. The power of meditation is the ability to clear the mind and energy in the body. The frustration is getting the mind and body to calm so the benefits can be enjoyed.

The meditation technique which is taught with this simple system is entirely user friendly, simple to master and takes only about 15 minutes. The use of the mind during the process keeps the unwanted fleeting and disruptive "monkey mind" thoughts out. The use of breathing and movement awakens the energy centers in the body and cleanses the entire physical and energetic body. Please reach out to receive your own personal introduction and recorded meditation through an MP3 Download Instructions are found at the end of the chapter.

For those that like verification of what is presented here. We have it. There has been a scale of consciousness that was developed by Dr. David Hawkins in his paradigm shifting book Power Vs. Force which allows a person to test their level of consciousness on a scale from 1 to 1000. With accurate muscle testing you can discern where your level of consciousness is and by following this simple system you can track the increases in your consciousness into full enlightenment.

Here is the fascinating and revolutionary discovery. The scale of consciousness has been altered. There is not a limit on consciousness as previously thought to be at 1000. There are now scores of people who possess verifiable levels of consciousness over 1000. This is unprecedented and is amazing and awe inspiring. Here is the best part of this. It is available and maintainable for anyone, yes anyone, who will follow this simple system. If you wish to obtain more information about the simple system and see the stories of those who have been on the journey of awakening to high conscious awareness, please visit the website of the author.

Let me tell you how all this was discovered. My interest has always been in healing but my job was real estate. While working in real estate my studies earned me a masters degree in Psychology, Consciousness, Health and Healing. During the real estate meltdown my company was crushed. At the worst possible time my car was smashed in a fatal crash where my life was spared. After three years and over a hundred physician visits an idea to use my mind came to me in a meditation. Immediately the bones began moving and in two weeks my recovery was complete. Wow!

Healing of the mind and emotions was next. Sitting for many months muscle testing every single issue until it was resolved resulted in a giant catalog of healing techniques sourced from me and later mastered on a large group of clients. As the healing occurred, the level of consciousness was going up, this was tracked by several clients who knew how to muscle test. As the consciousness increased we were all astounded all the while my personal challenges increased.

There were weeks of time where the body and mind were entirely useless. Retreat from the world seemed to be the only way to deal with it. My resolve to reach full enlightenment was firm and to overcome the tremendous issues. There was a time for months where even getting out of the house was an accomplishment. It was during this time that the concept of visiting energies was understood and it was discerned how to remove them. In a short time full body functioning had returned and the level of consciousness was beyond full enlightenment. During this time my clients began to rise quickly, some reached full enlightenment, then many.

A great discovery was made that the body holds on to consciousness termed "pathology" and that these could be removed with higher consciousness. This goal for myself and others became my next major devotion. The average client would come to me with at least 25 pathologies discerned through muscle testing. With consciousness work and the simple application of discipline we now see people enjoying life with only a few if any at all.

The group of people are now glowing examples of health, vitality and well-being. My life is from this time forward dedicated to serving those who wish to have such a transformation. The manner in which this is done is through group meditations, online classes, masterminds, live workshops as well as private coaching. Please contact me for further information.

3 Key Takeaways from this Chapter:

1) High conscious awareness, full enlightenment and complete healing is possible
2) A system insuring success is available, a step by step guide
3) Start by using the intention for enlightened consciousness, contemplate, muscle test and meditate to build your energy

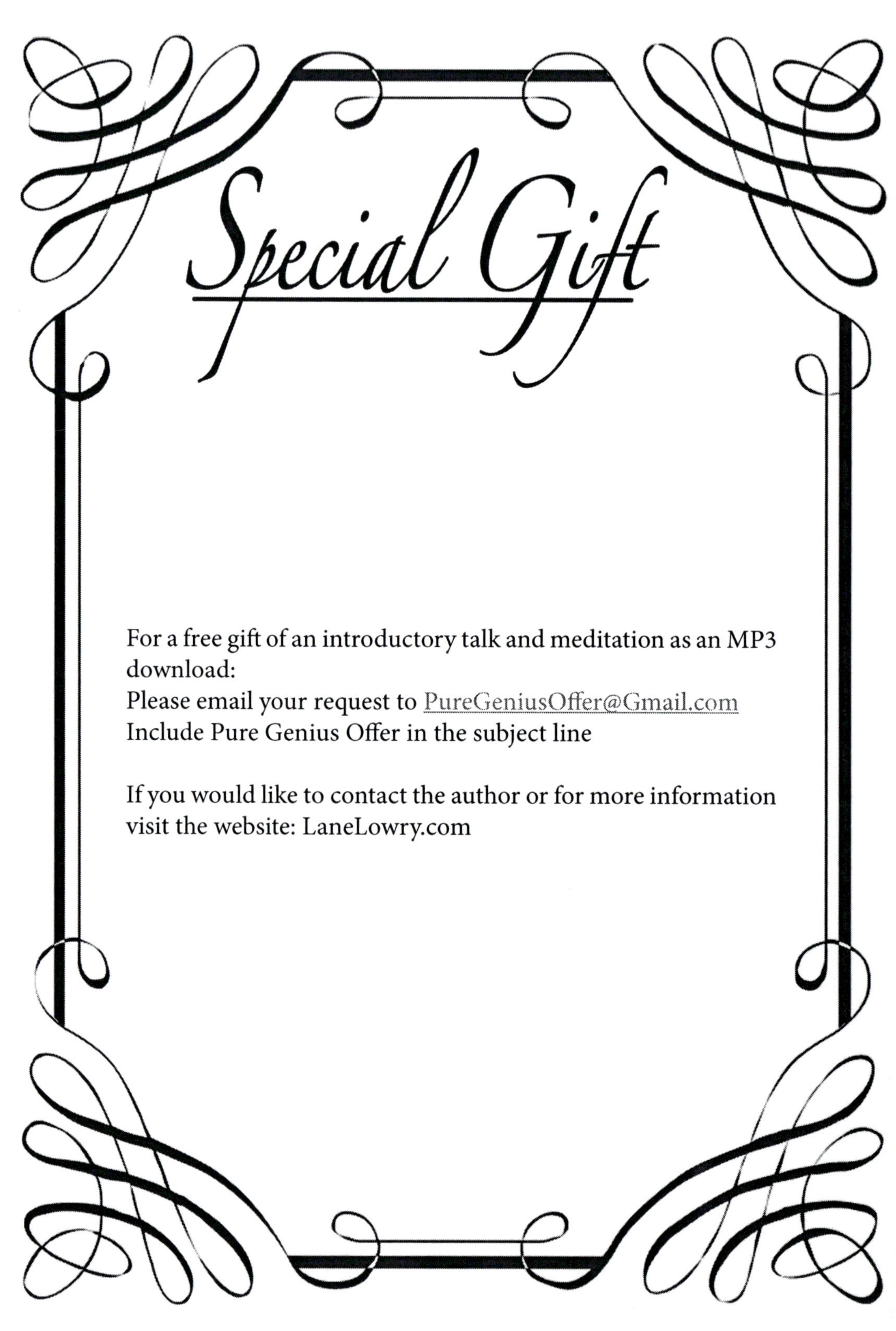

Special Gift

For a free gift of an introductory talk and meditation as an MP3 download:
Please email your request to PureGeniusOffer@Gmail.com
Include Pure Genius Offer in the subject line

If you would like to contact the author or for more information visit the website: LaneLowry.com

SCOTT WELLE

BIO:

Scott Welle is the founder of Scott Welle Transformations, a Minneapolis-based consulting company dedicated to enhancing health, happiness and high-performance. As an inspiring leader and in-demand speaker, trainer and coach, Scott has helped hundreds of people unlock their full potential through truth, motivation, guidance and quality education.

Scott started his career as a personal trainer in Minneapolis and was the top selling personal trainer in the nation three times for Wellbridge and Life Time Fitness. He went on to become the Regional Metabolic and Heart Rate Training Specialist for all Colorado Athletic Clubs.

Scott has a Master's degree in Kinesiology and numerous certifications in health-related fields. He serves on the Executive Certification Board for National Exercise and Sport Trainers Association and is on the Advisory Board for the Minnesota School of Business – Globe University. Recently, Scott created Outperform The Norm, a cutting-edge program that helps leaders increase effectiveness, improve performance and find fulfillment.

Scott has completed 17 marathons and 5 Ironman triathlons, and is considered a foremost authority on the advanced psychology and physiology of high performance…for people in all walks of life.

GENIUS PROFILE:

Name: Scott Welle
Biggest Challenge/Obstacle Overcome:
Completing 5 Ironman triathlons

Top 3 Favorite Foods:
Salmon
Peanut Butter
Carrot Cake

Top 3 Favorite Musicians:
U2
Neil Diamond
Goldfinger

Top 3 Favorite Places Visited:
Paris
San Francisco
Many Mountainous Places in CO

Bucket List Item Not Yet Accomplished:
Run a 100 mile race

Top 3 Role Models or Heroes:
My brother (Jason)
Jim Rohn
John Wooden

by Scott T. Welle

You have a norm that exists inside of you. An internal governor, if you will. It wants to keep you in that comfortable sweet spot of security where great risks are never taken and great mistakes are never made. Every time you want to slam the gas pedal and kick it into high gear, it pulls you back to steady.

Great accomplishments don't happen here. Days monotonously drag by and paychecks are collected. Your routine is busy but you can't remember the last time you were TRULY challenged. You're meeting the status quo. And nothing seems broken so why bother fixing it?

But we're not fixing anything. We're building it better.

An Outperformer exists inside of you.

Forget outperforming the societal norm. First, I'm not even sure what "that" is anymore. Second, if you're reading this, you're probably already above that curve. What I'm talking about is Outperforming YOUR norm. Living a life of success and satisfaction and abundance and excellence where limits are pushed and you go out saying, "wow, that was one helluva good ride."

Outperform the Norm is not your grandma's self-help program. It is the advanced psychological, physiological and behavioral conditioning principles I've discovered from my 12+ years working with high performing athletes and that I've personally used to complete 5 Ironman Triathlons and 17 marathons. This is about the next level. You, Outperforming. And it starts from the inside out.

I'm not telling you it is going to be easy. I'm telling you it's going to be worth it. Let's go.

The Outperformers Brain

The power of the human mind is incredible. It is estimated that the brain produces 70,000 thoughts each day. It can either be our greatest asset or our largest liability. It solely depends on how we use it.

Fact: The non-negotiable key component for Outperformers is mental mastery. You get nowhere without it.

Contrary to popular belief, thoughts don't randomly creep into our brain. We condition our psychology the same way we condition our physiology – through the repeated presence of stimuli to produce a desired effect.

Anytime I meet a new athlete, I ask them what percentage of their sport they think is mental (vs. skills, talents, etc.). I, then, ask them what percentage of their time they're currently devoting to mental training (I refer to it as "Brain Training").

Their answer is never enough.

What percentage of YOUR success is mental? How much time are you spending each day in Brain Training?

Is your answer enough?

Leading up to a key running race, I frequently do hard workouts alone. No music. No pacing partner. No social support. Just me out there, solo, with my thoughts.

Racing is a metaphor for life. You're never competing against anyone else as much as you're competing against yourself. And if you constantly need someone to motivate you, how in the heck are you ever going to get motivated when no one else is around?

Your personal standard of excellence is tested when you're alone. You can blow it off and take a short cut. Or make sure no one is watching and say "I'll try harder tomorrow." No one would ever know, would they?

But you'll know…and that is not an outperformer's mindset.

Outperforming Principle #1 – *ACE*
Attitude. Controls. Everything.

How many times have you said, "[fill in the blank] makes me SO mad!?"

Question: Who controls your thoughts?

Answer: You do! You make yourself SO mad *in response to* [fill in the blank].

The starting point to an outperforming psychology is taking ownership for every single thought, feeling and emotion you have. No excuses. No justifications. No rationalizations. No blaming. No negativity.

You have 100% control over your attitude. Make your attitude work for you.

Outperforming Principle #2 – *No matter what happens, your confidence goes up.*

Supreme confidence propels you to action and it starts with 3 things:

If I tank in a big race, it was my fault. Not the weather, not the race course, not the number of runners or my outfit – it was me. All me. I was in control of the outcome. We call this *Personalization*, which means you take personal accountability for the things that happen to you instead of attributing it to some external factor.

Next, people wonder all the time how basketball players can have a horrible game and miss every shot, then pull it together at the end to hit the game winner. Knowing that, even if something negative happens, it will not CONTINUE to happen, is called *Permanence*. Outperformers know the past doesn't dictate the future. Every second is a new, fresh opportunity.

The last key to confidence is *Pervasiveness*, which means if something negative happens in one area, it will not spill into other areas. It brings to mind a former running client of mine: Bad day at work, her running would suffer. Fight with her boyfriend, her running would suffer. Not enough Likes on her Facebook post, her running would suffer. Every negative thing that happened in her life spilled over and hurt her confidence as a runner. Outperformers keep their confidence by containing a negative to one area.

You show me ANY successful person (entrepreneur, executive, athlete, etc.); I'll show you someone with confidence. You'll go nowhere without it.

Outperforming Principle #3 – *Failure is not an option.*
Outperformers never fail. Ever. They know the only way they can fail is to not learn from the result or to not try at all. When something goes wrong, 'The Norm' sees failure. Outperformers see it as now knowing what not to do and being one step closer to success.

Studies have shown that, towards the end of life, one of the primary regrets people have is that they didn't take more risks. Making the safe play may seem like the commonsense thing to do, but this is why 'The Norm' is head bobbing at their desk all day and needing 8 cups of coffee to artificially stay energized. No fire in the belly. No passion in the heart.

How many passionate people do you know that play it safe? Probably none. They are passionate BECAUSE they take risks, challenge themselves and don't recognize failure. They are always moving forward. They want the ball in their hands to take the last shot.

Outperforming Principle #4 – *FEAR = False Evidence Appearing Real.*
When you peel back the layers and cut through the BS, fear is almost always the thing holding people back. But the majority of our fears are irrational.

Statistically speaking, 92% of what we fear will NEVER happen. So, why do we let it hold us back?

The difference is in perspective.

The Norm: Fear = "What if [insert negative statement]"

What if I fail? What if I'm not good enough? What if I'm not ready? What if this doesn't work? What if I don't know enough?

Outperformer: Fearlessness = "What if [insert negative statement]"

What if I succeed? What if I'm BETTER than enough? What if I'm prepared? What if this works perfectly? What if I know plenty?

This simple shift in mindset can change your life. Anytime a new situation arises, 'The Norm' will weigh the cons and then decide whether to act. Outperformers will weigh the pros and take massive action.

Outperforming Principle #5 – *Create a Personal Psychology of Excellence*

Outperformers hold themselves to a higher standard, produced more by effort and execution than by results. The former creates the latter.

Results come from trying harder and giving more effort. They also come from refining your skills and perfecting your craft.

Some call this 'intrinsic motivation.' It's not. Excellence is the reflection in the mirror that challenges you, questioning, "is that *really* all you've got?" It's the little voice inside your head that won't let you sleep unless you've busted your butt, gotten uncomfortable and accomplished something today.

It NEVER lets you settle.

You can see this in any great athlete or successful businessperson. It is not about perfection. It is about a personal pursuit of excellence. When you've embraced this psychology, you've lifted the governor. You're full speed ahead.

The Outperformers Body

Your body is a machine. It is a complex system that must be firing on all cylinders for peak performance. The better your body functions, the higher your quality of performance.

Fact: Garbage in equals garbage out. High-octane fuel in equals high-level performance out.

The physiology of our body determines our stress, energy, tension, mental clarity and recovery. Outperformers know that strengthening your body also strengthens your mind…and it strengthens your character. It makes you better in ALL aspects of your life.

To be clear, I'm not talking about getting ripped so you look good at the beach. That's great, but that's aesthetics. I'm talking about improving your unique physiological functioning so you can handle the demands necessary to outperform.

The body will adapt to whatever you want it to do. You may already be a high performer without exercise, sleep or decent nutrition. I see it all the time. Your body adapts and you're still able to function…very well in some cases.

But you'll never reach your potential this way. And I guarantee, you're paying for it in other ways (stress, aging, pain, hormonal levels, biomarkers).

You want to outperform? Build a better machine. Work it and it will work for you.

Outperforming Principle #1 – *You have no offseason.*

Your job is more difficult than a professional athlete's. They have an offseason and a set amount of time to rest and recover. Other than a couple vacations per year, you probably don't. You always have to be on. When the bell rings, you have to answer it.

Because of this, you need to build a body to last. You need stamina, endurance and durability to resist wear and tear. By doing this, you will be as strong at 4:30pm as you are at 8:30am. Or on Friday as you are on Monday.

You won't need two pots of coffee or supercharged energy drinks. Your improved physiology will take care of that naturally.

Outperforming Principle #2 – *You're in training.*

Outperformers train. What distinguishes training from exercise is that you have a specific method to your madness. Exercisers wander aimlessly around the gym, thinking, "I wonder what I should do today?" Time is usually wasted and very little progress is made.

When you train, you know *what* you're doing and *why* you're doing it. It's purposeful. You're there to make progress. You're there to achieve a specific result, efficiently and effectively.

Want a stronger body? Lift heavier weights. Want a stronger heart? Do more intense cardio. Want more stamina? Shorten your rest periods.

But challenge yourself! The same way going through the motions won't get it done in business, neither will it get it done in the gym. Push your body. Test your limits.

Outperforming Principle #3 – *Food is Fuel*

Food is not food. Food is fuel. Food is energy. All athletes and Outperformers understand this. You put a certain amount of fuel into your body; you get a certain amount of production out of it.

It starts with breakfast. You don't drive your car on an empty tank of gas; so don't drive your body on empty either. Putting fuel into your body within one hour of waking up kick starts your metabolism and sets the tone for your entire day.

Timing of fuel of important. Eat every 2-3 hours. Small portion sizes, frequently. Doing this keeps your energy levels up, your metabolism stoked, your insulin levels stable and your mental clarity focused (your brain consumes 25% of the body's nutrients for energy).

Type of fuel is also important. Lots of protein, complex carbs, vegetables, healthy fats and fruits. The less processed, the better. The less sodium, the better. The fewer ingredients, the better. And if you have to ask whether something is healthy, save yourself the breath. It isn't.

Outperforming Principle #4 – *The importance of hydration*

Fact: The single BEST thing you can do for your physiological function is to drink more water.

You cannot outperform when you're dehydrated. Your body is made up of 60-70 percent water and as little as 1-2 percent difference in dehydration will impair your ability to act, react and make decisions.

The brain control centers for thirst and hunger are also located right next to each other and it's common for us to mistake the two. Many times hunger doesn't actually *mean* we're hungry – it means we're dehydrated.

The starting point for hydration is 100 ounces of water per day. If you're not getting this amount, you're not optimally hydrated.

But there's more...

If you drink caffeine, alcohol, work out, live at altitude, or live in a warm climate, you need more water. 100 ounces is simply your baseline starting point.

Above and beyond this, hydration also helps with joint pain, flexibility, nutrient transport, detoxifying the body, better skin, metabolism and digestion.

Outperforming Principle #5 – *Recharge your batteries*

Think of your cell phone. It gets drained during the day and you recharge it at night. If you don't recharge it long enough, your battery never gets back to full. You're starting the day at less than full strength.

Your body is no different. When an athlete finishes a competition, they stretch, sit in a cold tub, replenish their nutrients and electrolytes, get a massage and rest as much as possible. They do this because they know their livelihood is predicated upon their ability to perform at full capacity. And without rejuvenation, both physically and mentally, their performance will suffer.

You do not need to be a professional athlete to take a page out of their playbook. Your ability to Outperform is directly proportional to your ability to stress, rest, adapt and bounce back stronger from a "competition," or a tough day at the office.

Everything you need is inside of you. You find confidence, excellence and answers by building your psychology. You find stamina, energy and strength by building your physiology. All it takes is the discipline, dedication and sacrifices to get it done.

Can you be successful and live a great life without these things? Absolutely. Can you live your BEST life and accomplish everything you're capable of accomplishing without these things? Not a chance.

Fact: If you keep doing what you've always done, you'll keep getting what you've always got.

For 12+ years, I've been obsessed with the study of human potential. Why? Because it's limitless. Uncapped. No one knows what we're capable of. It's a constant, never-ending search for higher.

I'm not trying to make you something you're not, but just know there's an Outperformer in you. And if you're serious about setting the new standard and accomplishing more than you ever thought possible, it starts now and it starts with you. No more dilly-dally mumbo-jumbo "I think I can" talk. You CAN. You WILL.

In Health, Happiness and High-Performance,

- Scott

3 Takeaways

1. Your ability to Outperform is directly proportional to your mental mastery. You cannot accomplish everything you're capable of if you haven't conditioned your psychology to make it happen.
2. Embracing a psychology of excellence means setting higher standards for yourself than anyone else can possibly set for you.
3. Your body is a machine. Build it strong, give it the right fuel and let it rest, and it will work amazingly for you.

Action Plan

1. Dedicate 20-30 minutes per day to developing your psychology. Read an inspiring book, watch a video, listen to a podcast in the car. First thing in the morning is best.
2. Complete the following sentence: "To live a life of excellence, I must..." *(don't overthink this, just write whatever comes to mind. But write at least 10 things. This is your starting point to becoming an Outperformer)*
3. Keep a 3-day food journal, writing down EVERYTHING you're eating, including how much water you're drinking. How does this align with the Outperformer's body? Are you fueling your body for performance?

Special Gift

In-depth, 3-part video training series (with downloadable workbook) on the advanced psychology, physiology and behavioral conditioning of Outperformers.

Go to: http://outperformthenorm.com/gift

CPSIA information can be obtained at www.ICGtesting.com
Printed in the USA
BVOW021915030613

322316BV00004B/12/P

9 781935 723974